Are you a true baseball fanatic? Do you ponder slugging percentages, mull over the purity of the designated hitter, and mourn over a blown double play? Do you study names, intricacies, statistics—every niche and nuance of the game? Are you an armchair addict, a box score buff, a bleacher bum? The true fan, with an extended knowledge of baseball lore, knows names, facts, feats, and events. Here's your chance to show your stuff.

What pitcher did Hank Aaron victimize when he hit home run #715?

What Hall of Famer in 1933 ended the Yankees' record of 308 consecutive games without being shut out?

What is the only park that was called home by three different major league teams in this century?

Designed like baseball itself, this extraordinary quiz book tests the fanatic in every phase of the sport. It offers an incredible variety of questions based not on an ability to memorize obscure facts, but on true knowledge of the game. Its unique scoring system awards hits and RBIs for correct answers, allowing for an accurate judge of your baseball know-how in comparison to others. It's challenging, it's fun, it's a hit, it's . . .

THE MOST EXTRAORDINARY BASEBALL QUIZ BOOK EVER

⊘ **SIGNET** (0451)

THE WORLD OF SPORTS

☐ **THE MOST EXTRAORDINARY BASEBALL QUIZ BOOK, EVER by David Nemec.** Are you a true baseball fanatic? Do you study every niche and nuance of the game? Well, watch out for curveballs as you test your knowledge on over 700 tantalizing questions that will prove what a true baseball scholar you are. (164504—$3.50)

☐ **THE ILLUSTRATED SPORTS RECORD BOOK (Updated and Revised Edition) by Zander Hollander and David E. Schulz.** Here, in a single book, are 350 records with stories and photos so vivid they'll make you feel that "you are there." Once and for all you'll be able to settle your sports debates on who holds what records and how he, or she, did it.

(157435—$3.95)

☐ **GREAT BASEBALL FEATS, FACTS & FIRSTS by David Nemec.** Thousands of scores, stats and stories in one amazingly complete volume! Discover the unconventional records, the offbeat feats, the historic scores and the one-of-a-kind characters that keep baseball flying—in this comprehensive up-to-the-minute encyclopedia. (161246—$4.95)

☐ **TENNIS, ANYONE? by Dick Gould, famed tennis coach.** Superb instructional photographs and diagrams of strokes and strategy . . . "A magnificent job . . . this book is a must!"—Pancho Segura, all-time great player and coach to Jimmy Connors (159284—$4.95)

☐ **THE GOLFER'S STROKE SAVING HANDBOOK by Craig Shankland, Dale Shankland, Dom Lupo and Roy Benjamin.** For the amateur and the weekend golfer, the closest thing to a series of playing lessons from a pro. How to hit the best possible shot in any kind of situation, plus vital tips for all the strokes with advice relating to both technique and terrain. All tested and proven. (155378—$4.50)

*Prices slightly higher in Canada

Buy them at your local bookstore or use this convenient coupon for ordering.

NEW AMERICAN LIBRARY
P.O. Box 999, Bergenfield, New Jersey 07621

Please send me the books I have checked above. I am enclosing $_____
(please add $1.00 to this order to cover postage and handling). Send check or money order—no cash or C.O.D.'s. Prices and numbers are subject to change without notice.

Name_____

Address_____

City _____ State _____ Zip Code _____

Allow 4-6 weeks for delivery.

This offer, prices and numbers are subject to change without notice.

The Most
Extraordinary
Baseball
Quiz Book
Ever

David Nemec

A SIGNET BOOK

NEW AMERICAN LIBRARY

A DIVISION OF PENGUIN BOOKS USA INC.

NAL BOOKS ARE AVAILABLE AT QUANTITY DISCOUNTS WHEN USED TO PROMOTE
PRODUCTS OR SERVICES. FOR INFORMATION PLEASE WRITE TO PREMIUM MARKET-
ING DIVISION, NEW AMERICAN LIBRARY, 1633 BROADWAY, NEW YORK, NEW
YORK 10019.

Copyright © 1990 by David Nemec

All rights reserved

SIGNET TRADEMARK REG. U.S. PAT. OFF. AND FOREIGN COUNTRIES
REGISTERED TRADEMARK—MARCA REGISTRADA
HECHO EN DRESDEN, TN, U.S.A.

SIGNET, SIGNET CLASSIC, MENTOR, ONYX, PLUME, MERIDIAN
and NAL BOOKS are published by New American Library, a division of
Penguin Books USA Inc., 1633 Broadway, New York, New York 10019

First Printing, March, 1990

1 2 3 4 5 6 7 8 9

PRINTED IN THE UNITED STATES OF AMERICA

Contents

Introduction   vii

APRIL

Opening Day Classic   13
1. Fabled Freshmen   14
2. Moments to Remember   16
3. Glorious Glovemen   19
4. Death in the Afternoon   21
5. Team Teasers   23
6. Black Is Beautiful   25
7. Their Niche Is Secure   28

MAY

Southpaw Surprise   33
8. Moments to Remember   33
9. Great Goats and Victims   36
10. South of the Border   39
11. Minor League Maestros   41
12. Super Siblings   45
13. Their Niche Is Secure   47
14. Whatever Happened to . . . ?   49

JUNE

Leader of the Pack   55
15. Team Teasers   56
16. Now Batting for . . .   58
17. Moments to Remember   61
18. Glorious Glovemen   63
19. Like Father Like Son   66
20. World War II Wrinkles   68
21. Their Niche Is Secure   70

JULY

Rapid Robert's Redux   **77**
22. Moments to Remember   78
23. North of the Border   80
24. Super Siblings   83
25. Great Goats and Victims   85
26. Forget Me Not   87
27. Their Niche Is Secure   93
28. Minor League Maestros   95

AUGUST

The Magic Year   **103**
29. Black Is Beautiful   104
30. Fabled Freshmen   106
31. Moments to Remember   109
32. Team Teasers   111
33. The Evolving Game   114
34. Men of Mystery   116
35. Their Niche Is Secure   121

SEPTEMBER

Only Yesterday   **127**
36. Like Father Like Son   128
37. South of the Border   130
38. World War II Wrinkles   133
39. Now Batting for . . .   135
40. Their Niche is Secure   137
41. Glorious Glovemen   140
42. Minor League Maestros   142

OCTOBER

Forgotten Series Hero   **149**
43. October Heroes   150
44. Their Niche Is Secure   152
45. October Heroes   155
46. North of the Border   157
47. Great Goats and Victims   160
48. Death in the Afternoon   162
49. October Heroes   164

Answers   169

Introduction

How dare I call this the most extraordinary baseball quiz book ever?

Well, first and foremost, it's been designed to give you, my fellow buff, the three things you most want when you put your expertise on the line: fun, a keen challenge and, perhaps above all, a sense that you're learning something new about the game you love. In short, you're not only looking to match wits, you also like to come away from a book like this with the feeling that you've been enriched into the bargain.

You will be, guaranteed, by the time you finish here. What I've assembled is a full season's worth of entertainment, April through October, over 100 questions in each month, starting off with rookies and ending with post-season heroes. There's a logic to that, of course, as there is to all the categories I've chosen. Indeed, I'll warn you right up front that to score well you need to be moderately savvy in every phase of the game's rich history.

That isn't to say, though, that you've got to have a raft of stats and a host of obscure players at your fingertips. Actually, top marks can be achieved by anyone who has a fair smattering of knowledge coupled with a good eye for sifting out the right answer to even the most seemingly impossible question if given a few helpful clues.

Before illustrating how I work, let me first show you an example of the type of question I loath: What pitcher was beaten by a ninth-inning grand slam four times while working the second game of a doubleheader? Trivia at its worst. If you don't happen to know the pitcher off the top of your head, there's nothing in the question to help you nail him. More than that, are you really interested in finding out the answer? I wouldn't be. But tell me that those four games were the only ones that pitcher started in his career and my ears suddenly perk up. Then add that he pitched for 12 seasons, once led the National League in saves, and gave up no other grand slams in his career—and all my burners are fired.

See what I mean? A good question doesn't just hit you with a bizarre feat. It offers you a reasonable shot at getting the player who performed it by providing enough other information about him to make for at least an educated guess.

No, to my knowledge, there's no such pitcher who was victimized by grand slams only in twin-bill nightcaps, nor are all the questions in this book constructed like the one about him. Many of them are accompanied by only a single clue and some by none at all when the panel feels that only a downright novice should need help.

In any case, here I am at work on three different levels of questions.

SIMPLE: He became the first pitcher in history to notch 4,000 career strikeouts when he fanned Danny Heep in 1984.

MEDIUM: Many analysts consider Ernie Shore's perfect game tainted because he came on in relief of Babe Ruth and faced only 26 batters. Whose perfect game was tainted with what would have been a single if a Cleveland batter who stroked a clean hit to right field had not been thrown out at first base by Lon Knight?

TOUGH: He is the only player to lead either major circuit in fewest strikeouts despite having the lowest batting average of any regular (400+ at-bats) in his league that season. Your clues are that he fanned ten times and hit .221 while playing beside a rookie second baseman who that year became the first player from an expansion team to be league leader in walks.

All right, question No. 1 is so easy, it requires no discussion.

In No. 2 you're a heavy favorite to score if you either know what team Lon Knight played right field for—not likely—or else who pitched a perfect game against a

Cleveland team (it's only been done once). At worst, you're made to guess, and the odds are that even if you come up short, you're not terribly crushed. You just learned something, right? Or did you already know there was once a perfect game that had what ought to have been a base hit?

The clues in No. 3 tell you that our man was either a first baseman—highly improbable—or a shortstop, that he played for an expansion club and that he had quite an extraordinary teammate since precious few rookies are league leaders in walks. Still, with all that, you're a long shot to get him because it's a rugged question, no two ways about it. But again, you learned something intriguing—a player who was at once the hardest in his league to strike out and its worst hitter—unless you're the one maven in a million to whom odd record combinations have no appeal.

I won't spoil your fun by giving the answers to our sample questions. Consider them a bonus or, if you will, a teaser. And incidentally, you can expect to be teased and cajoled throughout this test, sometimes by clues given in the form of puns or what seem to be merely idle comments. In any event, the book is full of 714 questions just like the sample ones, about the same number of at-bats you'd get in a season if you were in there for all 162 games. You're invited thereby, as you go along, to keep score of your hits, extra bases, and RBIs and then figure out your final stats. Don't expect to hit above .300, though, unless you really know your stuff. This is the big league of baseball memorabilia, after all.

Now enjoy.

April

Opening Day Classic

Tickets for Detroit's inaugural game in the American League, against the Milwaukee Brewers on April 25, 1901, were sold out weeks in advance. The Tigers' first home, tiny Bennett Field, which seated only 6,000, was ringed in addition with over 4,000 standees when the opening pitch was thrown, swelling the total paid crowd to 10,023, a stunning figure for that time in Detroit, then among the smallest cities on the big league map.

After all the ballyhoo the opener in the new major league had received, it at first promised to be a terrible bust. Milwaukee shot off to a quick 7–0 lead, scoring twice in the second inning on one hit and four errors, and five times in the third frame to drive Detroit's vaunted rookie pitching ace from the box.

By the bottom of the ninth inning, the Brewers had extended their lead to 13–4 and seemed certain to bring their star center fielder and future Hall of Famer a victory in his managerial debut. The Tigers proceeded, however, to fashion the greatest Opening Day comeback in history by rallying for ten runs in their last turn at bat. The hero of this incredible last-ditch effort was Detroit's first baseman, who cracked two doubles in the ninth inning alone and four on the day, an American League record that not only was set at the very beginning of the loop's existence but has never been surpassed. The first sacker's second ninth-inning double, with two out, also proved to be the game-winning hit when it plated Doc Casey and Kid Gleason.

For a two-run double of your own, name the Tigers' slugging gateway guardian that day. Take an extra base, plus another RBI, if you also know the Brewers' Hall of Fame player-manager who helplessly watched victory disappear when the game-winning two-bagger sailed over his head into the throng of outfield standees.

Claim a grand slam homer if, in addition, you can identify the Tigers' rookie starter, who was kayoed early on in this classic opener. He won 23 games that season and logged a frosh-record 35 complete games in his 36 starts—failing to finish only his, and his team's, opening assignment!

1. Fabled Freshmen

You start off as a raw recruit in this book until you prove, as all of these men swiftly did, that you belong in top company.

1. Loosen up with an easy single by naming the 19-year-old phenom who set a new rookie record when he netted 276 strikeouts in 1984.

2. Naming the only hurler to cop both rookie honors and a Cy Young Award as a frosh should lead to another cinch single.

3. A fairly tough double if you know the A's lefty who won 20 games as a yearling, but lost the rookie award to Roy Sievers. The year it happened rates an RBI even if you goof and name the wrong A's portsider of that vintage.

4. Let's play "what if" for a moment. There was no rookie award when Ty Cobb was a frosh, but if there had been, the honor in all probability would have gone to what Brownie outfielder who led the AL in hits that year? When I add that he later won a bat crown, you'll feel you've pulled a real rock if you don't score an RBI two-bagger here.

5. When he bagged the Rookie of the Year prize, he became the first Seattle Mariner to win a major award. Even a chipmunk should know this for a single.

6. We all know that Mark McGwire now holds the record for the most home runs by a frosh, but who still has the mark for the most extra-base hits? Take a triple if you know the man who took Harley Boss's job.

7. In 1987 Benito Santiago broke his all-time rookie hitting-streak record of 27 games, set with the 1899 Pirates. Even with the clue that our man also established the all-time frosh mark for the most triples that season, you'll have to be sharp to collect a two-run double here.

8. The shortest man ever to win a Rookie of the Year Award, he was also the first to be chosen from a last-place team. Either of those two clues should suffice to get you in safely with a bunt single.

9. He is the only Rookie of the Year winner to lead a minor league in home runs the same season he copped frosh honors. A single for him and two RBIs if you know the circuit he topped in homers before being called up.

10. A two-bagger's yours if you can nail the only rookie record holder—for both the highest batting average and the highest slugging average, no less—who began the season in the minors with Rochester of the International League. Plus an RBI for knowing the year he skyrocketed.

11. Just a single for the outfielder-DH who copped AL rookie honors in 1980 after he clubbed 23 homers and hit .289, but never again played regularly.

12. He was the first player on an expansion team to win a Rookie of the Year honor. Only clue you should need is that his 16 victories set a club record that was broken the following year by another frosh sensation, who had 19 wins. RBI single.

13. For a two-run double, name the Tigers' first sacker who holds the AL rookie record for the most hits in a 154-game season, plus an extra RBI for the year he did it.

14. He set a new all-time yearling mound record when he appeared in 80 games in 1986. Works out to be only a single, but treat yourself to an RBI if you also know the team he pitched for.

15. Only the 1937 Boston Braves and one other team in this century have had *two* rookie 20-game winners. The team alone will earn a double; the team and the year it happened raise this to a homer; take an extra RBI if you know *either* of the team's frosh sensations; and a grand slam should you be astute enough to snare the whole package.

16. In 1926 this Cincinnati fly-chaser narrowly missed becoming the first rookie in the 20th century to win a batting title when he hit .350. Cut after he started slowly in 1927, he later starred in the AA and PCL. Historians would consider me loony if I rated this one more than an RBI triple.

SCORING CHART

Potential Total Bases: 28	At-Bats: 16
	Hits:
Potential RBIs: 17	RBIs:
	Total Bases:

2. Moments to Remember

Experts will gobble up just about everything put on the table in this category, for we're dealing here only with the game's staples— its greatest players and moments.

1. He once had a season in which he led his league in errors at his position, strikeouts, and grounding into double plays. What's so great about it is that he was named the MVP that year. A rather wicked double.

2. The 1894 Phillies, perhaps the greatest hitting team ever, were doomed to also-ran status when their star shortstop was beaned. Without his stellar glove they were forced to employ Joe Sullivan, a marginal fielder. Our man, later a club owner in the Southern Association, was so severely injured he didn't return to the game until 1897. Two-run homer.

3. In 1927 he became both the oldest and the last pitcher in major league history to hurl two complete games in one day when he split a twin bill for the Phillies. Hard enough to earn an RBI double.

4. On April 23, 1964, he became the lone pitcher in this century to lose a complete-game nine-inning no-hitter when his Colt-45s were edged 1–0 by the Reds. RBI single.

5. In 1985 he scored 146 runs to become the first since 1949 to tally that many. Just a scratch bingle—and a loud laugh if you miss it.

6. The MVP Award was given for 16 years before he became the first player at his position to cop the honor. Two for his name; an RBI for his position.

7. One year short of his 40th birthday, he became the oldest ever to win an MVP Award. A single for his name; an RBI for the year he did it.

8. Close followers of the game weren't amazed when this Hall of Famer, at age 52, caught the full nine innings of the game that clinched the 1904 NL flag. They knew he'd already worked 65 games for Bridgeport in the Connecticut League that year and could

have predicted he'd still be hale enough to play 93 games two years later for the same club. Rates only a single.

9. He hit .322 in 1928, his first of 18 seasons as a regular, the highest average ever achieved by a teenager in big-league garb. Single.

10. This Hall of Famer failed to cop his third Triple Crown when he lost a batting title by .00016 of a point. Single for his name; an RBI for the year it happened; and another RBI for knowing who robbed him at the wire.

11. He is the only player in this century to have a four-homer game in a losing cause. Easy single.

12. After 12 years in the majors this former battery mate of Walter Johnson's had only six home runs and had once gone five seasons without a circuit clout. Upon winning the Cardinals' catching job in 1922, he exemplified the impact the lively ball had had on the game when he zapped 13 homers and hit .293. Two-run homer.

13. Here's your grand slam for today. All you have to do is name the lone member of the champion 1936 U.S. Olympic baseball team to make the majors. What's so hard about it? Well, he won only one game up top, that with the 1943 Giants.

14. The first great Italian pitcher in major league history burst onto the scene in 1946 and posted the third of three successive 20-win seasons in 1951. That clue alone should steer you off Sal Maglie. Take two here.

SCORING CHART

Potential   At-Bats: 14
Total Bases: 28

                                   Hits:

Potential
RBIS: 14   RBIS:

                                   Total Bases:

3. Glorious Glovemen

Defensive stars get short shrift now, but there was a time when fielding averages were considered more important than batting averages. For this to be a true historical test, I'd be remiss indeed if I didn't try your knowledge of the great glovemen, some of whom, in fact, never even played with a glove.

1. Excluding pitchers, the only career fielding-average record not held by a player active after 1977 belongs to whom? Only a single for this glove ace who starred in the town where he was born.

2. Vastly underrated in his time and nearly unknown now, he was the first shortstop to play ten or more seasons and retire with a career fielding average above .970. Last seen with the 1950 Cardinals, he's worth a double.

3. Among third basemen with the top ten career FAs, only two were active prior to 1940. Triple if you get both; down to a sac hit if you know just one.

4. This Hall of Famer holds the mark for the highest career FA by a pitcher. That clue given earlier in the game reduces this to a run-scoring double.

5. He was the first catcher to handle 9500 career chances. Now, if you know anything at all about what accounts for the bulk of the catchers' chances, you

surely won't blow this shot at a three-bagger by guessing somebody like Ray Schalk.

6. He is the only catcher ever to collect fewer than 500 putouts in more than 150 games. For the expert this should be a bargain homer—very few catchers have worked more than 150 games in a season and fewer still have done it in an era when K's (which of course are what account for the bulk of a catcher's putouts and total chances), were scarce.

7. He was the first catcher to total 1,100+ putouts in a season. Obviously, knowing something about team pitching strikeout records will help score a two-run single here.

8. He leads all outfielders in career assists and chances. Easy bingle.

9. His 44 assists in 1930 are the most by any outfielder since 1893. Two-bagger.

10. Among the top 15 outfielders in career assists, only he was active after 1930. And not very long after 1930, either; that clue plus being told that he began as a pitcher makes you a strong candidate to triple here.

11. He was the first outfielder in this century to lead his league in FA three consecutive seasons. Hint: he tied for the top spot twice. Bigger hint: he played for a manager who believed only a select few regulars should play more than about 120 games a year. Still, for all that, I'll give a homer.

12. This second sacker set a season record that stood for 23 years when he fielded .978 in 1896. The clue that it was one of the first seasons in his long career that he played with a glove pares this down to a run-scoring single.

13. The longest-standing season FA record belongs to this Giants star who fielded .983 way back in 1924. For a single name him and take an RBI for knowing the position at which he still holds the all-time NL mark.

14. His nine seasons as a league leader in fielding top the list among first basemen. Nope, not Garvey or Stuffy McInnis. In fact, this one's hard enough to go for a two-run double.

15. He took part in a record 194 double plays in 1949 as his team, the A's, collected an all-time record 217 twin kills. You really shouldn't need any more clues than that to net an RBI double, but I'll tell you anyway that he has one of the highest career on-base percentages in history.

SCORING CHART

Potential Total Bases: 32	At-Bats: 15
	Hits:
Potential RBIS: 10	RBIS:
	Total Bases:

4. Death in the Afternoon

I used to think as a kid that I was fairly alone in my fascination with the Eddie Grants and the Mickey Finns and the Tiny Bonhams. But now that I've been around other baseball nuts awhile, it seems safe to venture that we've all got a special pantheon in our minds for the athletes who died young.

1. Get off the mark with a quick single by naming the lone player to die from an injury sustained in a regular-season major league game.

2. What happened to him has happened a number of times in the minors, though. For one, this inaptly named minor leaguer who'd been the Reds regular third baseman in 1913 was in the Southern Association two years later, trying to work his way back up top, when he was killed by a pitch thrown by Shotgun Rogers of Nashville, who later was on the same Yankees team with Carl Mays. Even with that bizarre connection and my helpful adverb you'll have to dig to score an inside-the-park homer.

3. A plane crash claimed this smooth-fielding Cubs second sacker and former NL Rookie of the Year early in 1964 only months after he'd completed his sophomore season. RBI single.

4. What two-time NL batting champion died after the 1924 season from surgical complications attributed in part to the aftereffects of a beaning he incurred during that campaign? Double.

5. Typhoid fever claimed this star Brooklyn second sacker in May 1892 after he'd suffered a near-fatal collision the previous season with teammate Oyster Burns while chasing a pop fly. Two-run homer.

6. He set the NL rookie winning-percentage record in 1910 when he chalked up a 20–4 mark with the Cubs. Four years later, by then a Yankee, he gave up Babe Ruth's first major league hit. Less than 18 months after that he was dead of tuberculosis. RBI double.

7. After two outstanding years with the Twins, this outfielder signed as a free agent with the Angels and was shot to death during a road trip with them late in the 1978 season. Gamble an RBI bingle you've forgotten him already.

8. The Phils regular receiver in 1929, he was killed that fall by a truck that jumped onto the sidewalk where he was strolling near his Baltimore home. Two-run homer.

9. He did a fine job in the Houston bullpen after being told in 1963 that he had cancer, but succumbed just as the following season was getting underway. RBI double.

10. End with a single by naming the only former AL MVP winner to die while still an active player.

SCORING CHART

Potential Total Bases: 22	At-Bats: 10
	Hits:
Potential RBIS: 9	RBIS:
	Total Bases:

5. Team Teasers

1. Despite two postponed games that were not made up, they set an all-time major league record in 1906 with 116 wins. Hard to believe there could be somebody out there who might not snare this simple single.

2. After tumbling into the cellar in 1914, this team set an AL record when it went 55 years before finishing in last place again. RBI single—and a second RBI for knowing the club's manager in 1969.

3. They set a record when they clinched their division in the 142nd game of the season—or with 20 games yet to be played. Single for the team; RBI if you nail the year too.

4. Playing a 140-game schedule, they won the flag by a record 27½ games. Double for the team; RBI for the year; another RBI if you know their hill leader whose departure meant they'd win by only 6½ games the following year.

5. They were the first team in major league history to be owned by a woman. Double for the team; make it a homer if you know the year she took over the club; and a three-run job if you also know her name.

6. From a .196 winning percentage, they vaulted to a pennant the following year to become the only team in major league history to spring from rock bottom to the top in a 12-month period. Two bases for the team; two ribbies for the years they went from the basement to the penthouse.

7. They are the only team in major league history with three 40-homer men. Single for the team and at least two of its bammers; RBI single if you know all three.

8. They were the first expansion team to occupy sole possession of first place as late as July 4. Two bases for the team, an RBI for the year.

9. Their 26 consecutive wins in 1916 tied a major league mark set by the 1875 Boston Red Caps. But while the Red Caps romped to the National Association pennant, they could do no better than fourth place. Single.

10. On April 30, 1986, when Roger Clemens fanned a record 20 batters in a game, among the men he faced were a free-swinger who set a new AL whiff mark for third baseman and a rookie who fanned 157 times. Who were they and what K-plagued team did they play for? You need it all for an RBI single.

11. In 1957 Lou Boudreau and Harry Craft took turns managing the first team in history without a pitcher who worked enough innings to qualify for the ERA crown when staff leader _____ had only 145. Double for the team; three ribbies for its "workhorse."

12. They defeated the Cincinnati Red Stockings 8–7 in 11 innings on June 14, 1870, to end Cincinnati's

record skein of 131 consecutive games without a loss. Triple for the team; three ribbies if you know the Cinci second sacker who blew what seemed a sure double-play ball to hand it the game.

13. In 1987 they became the only team in major league history to start the season with ten or more consecutive wins and yet fail to cop at least a division flag. Routine single.

14. Name the minor league club that won an Organized Baseball record seven consecutive pennants between 1919-25. One base for the team; an RBI for the league it dominated; another RBI if you know the owner-manager who assembled this dynasty.

15. Their first home ground was Hilltop Park, but that was only one of the reasons they were originally nicknamed the Highlanders. Going for just a single, but it rates two RBIs if you know who was at their helm in their first game at Hilltop.

SCORING CHART

Potential
Total Bases: 24

At-Bats: 15

Hits:

Potential
RBIS: 23

RBIS:

Total Bases:

6. Black Is Beautiful

1. He is the only black player to win a major league Triple Crown. Single.

2. He was the first black to win a World Series game. RBI double.

3. He was the only man prior to Burt Shotton to manage black players in the major leagues. Worth a homer, but credit a single if you know the team he managed and a sac hit if you know just the two black brothers who played for him.

4. Considered to be the first notable black player in America, he never made the majors, but starred off and on for nearly two decades in several minor leagues in the Midwest. Two-run double for this second sacker.

5. Unlike Ray Dandridge, this long-time Negro League star managed to make a few token major league appearances with the Giants. The PCL was where he left his stamp on OB, however, leading that circuit in hitting in 1949 and five times collecting over 200 hits. Slightly built, he had little power but was a deft base thief and a fine shortstop. RBI triple.

6. He was the first black to pitch for the St. Louis Cardinals. Solo homer.

7. What was the last position to be played by a black performer in an All-Star game? Single for the position; RBI if you know the first man to play it; another RBI for the year he did it.

8. What is the only position that as yet has produced no black Hall of Famers who played in the majors? A little thought should net an easy bingle.

9. He was the first black pitcher to be a 20-game winner. Two-bagger.

10. He was the first black pitcher to be a league leader in strikeouts. Bet a toothpick I can cause you to miss another double by enticing you into going for the wrong fireballer.

11. He is the only black player to hit .350+ with at least 20 homers and 100 RBIs for an AL team. Guaran-

teed, a whole lot of you will miss out on an RBI double because you've forgotten his super season.

12. He hit .202 for Fort Worth of the Texas League in 1955 after making 60 errors at shortstop for Pueblo of the Western League the previous year. His early minor league failings notwithstanding, in 1962 he led the NL in triples and set a new modern major league record (since broken) in another offensive department. Ample clues for the savvy to collect an RBI single.

13. What was the first year that every team in one of the major leagues had at least one black regular? Real tough without some clues, so I'll note that the circuit's batting leader that season was a former college All-American in another sport. Double for the right year *and* league.

14. Three major league teams were integrated in 1947. One of them, however, never had a black regular until after the franchise moved. Name that team for an RBI double; snag two more RBIs for the franchise's first black regular.

15. Lee Stanton's Seattle club home run record of 27, set in 1977, was broken two years later by what other black player functioning mainly as a DH? RBI single.

SCORING CHART

Potential Total Bases: 30	At-Bats: 15
	Hits:
Potential RBIS: 13	RBIS:
	Total Bases:

7. Their Niche Is Secure

Everybody here at one time held a significant major
league or OB record. Indeed, most of these men still
hold the top marks for at least a particular era, and many
are all-time standard bearers that you surely ought to
know if you covet that expert's badge.

1. He set an all-time mark with Detroit in 1887 when he
   had 166 RBIs in a 126-game season for an average of
   nearly 1⅓ ribbies per game. Yeah, he's in the Hall of
   Fame, but you won't be if you stumble trying for two
   bases here.

2. Ty Cobb and only one other player in OB history
   had over 300 career triples; the other man had more
   than 300 in the majors alone. Single.

3. His 135 career triples are the most by any player
   active exclusively since 1961, the beginning of the
   expansion era. Single.

4. He easily rates as the lefty with the best control since
   the advent of the lively ball in 1920; only once in his
   11 seasons did he give up as many as 49 bases on
   balls, that in 1973 with the Yankees. Only a single
   after all those clues.

5. He issued 179 walks in 1949, the most ever by an AL
   lefty. Considered a fine hitter for a pitcher, he belied
   it by garnering just six safeties in 80 career pinch-hit
   at-bats, including but one in 18 at-bats in 1953; that
   one, however, was a game-winning grand slam for
   the White Sox. Two-bagger.

6. This Hall of Famer set a modern record when he
   walked 218 batters in 1893, the first year the mound
   was at its present distance from home plate. RBI
   double.

7. His record in the minors was an undistinguished 47–41, but upon reaching the majors in 1937 at age 30 he produced an unparalleled .717 career winning percentage (109–43) and twice led the AL in ERA, including his finale in 1947. By adding that the team he played for had much to do with his success, I shave this down to an RBI single.

8. He is the only pitcher in this century to make 50 or more starts in a season. The clue that he also had the most gigantic season of any hurler in the 20th century narrows this one too down to just a single.

9. The only infielder in this century to hit two home runs in his first major league game, he played every position on the diamond for Kansas City in 1965. RBI single.

10. He had more career RBIs than all but two other players in NL history, yet never once led the senior circuit in RBIs. May require some thought, but once you hit on the answer you'll agree it's only worth a single.

11. He collected 1,314 RBIs without ever having more than 82 in a season and holds the record for the most career RBIs of any player who never topped the 100 mark. Still just a single.

12. In a career spanning just 14 full seasons and parts of three others he amassed nearly 2,000 RBIs. The antithesis of the above man and yet another single.

13. He's the only Cy Young winner who never won 20 games in a season and retired with a career winning percentage below .480. RBI two-bagger.

14. He's the oldest player ever to homer in an AL game; he led the NL in saves when he was 48; he started and won the Federal League's opening game, was a teammate of both Willie Keeler and Van Lingle

Mungo, posted 247 wins and 59 saves—and a solo homer says that even with all that, you'll draw a blank.

15. He's the only player ever to lead his league in RBIs and fielding with a perfect 1.000 FA that same season. Two-run double, and an extra ribby for the year he did it. Want more clues? Okay, he wasn't a shortstop.

SCORING CHART

Potential
Total Bases: 23

Potential
RBIS: 17

At-Bats: 15

Hits:

RBIS:

Total Bases:

May

Southpaw Surprise

In the fall of 1976, a certain 26-year-old lefthander who had been bouncing around his team's organization for years without distinguishing himself was nearly left unprotected in the expansion draft to stock the new Seattle and Toronto franchises. The following spring, the team's manager became so exasperated with his floundering pitcher that he said, "Show me somebody you can get out and I'll let you pitch to him."

For several weeks after the 1977 season began, the beleaguered southpaw saw no action. Finally, his skipper, depleted of lefthanded relief pitchers one spring night against Kansas City, had to bring in the club's doghouse denizen to face George Brett with the score tied and a runner on second. Brett instantly lined a single to center, but the runner hesitated just long enough for Mickey Rivers to throw him out at the plate. The lefty completed the last two innings of the game without incident, his team scored, and he earned his first major league victory. Our man proceeded to win 15 more games that season and the Cy Young Award the following year, but he has since said, "If it hadn't been for Mickey's throw, that might have been the end of me right there."

For a single, name the portsider who burst from the doghouse to stardom—and take an extra base if you also know the manager whose patience he nearly exhausted.

8. Moments to Remember

1. The Tigers would much rather have had Jack Morris or Doyle Alexander available to start the most crucial game of the 1987 regular season, but this lefty proved to be more than the Blue Jays could handle

when he flipped a 1–0 shutout and brought Detroit one of the greatest come-from-behind division flag wins in history. Single.

2. Phillies pitchers prevented him from becoming the youngest home run leader in history when they gave him five intentional walks in the last game of the 1929 season to assure their teammate, Chuck Klein, of the crown. Two-bagger.

3. He began the 1959 season with a 17–0 record and extended his consecutive wins streak to 22—all in relief—before losing his next-to-last decision to finish at 18–1. RBI single.

4. This outfielder stroked a mighty .211 for San Antonio of the Texas League in 1942, the year before he made the majors, and rapped a lusty .216 for Seattle of the PCL in 1954, the year after he exited from the majors. During his ten-year sojourn up top he was among the worst pinch hitters in history (15 for 120)—yet he also somehow contrived to hit .325 or better twice. Two-run triple, which should be a snap for all who know San Antonio's parent club in the '40s.

5. On their 30th birthdays these three future 300-game winners had only 190 wins among them—or an average of a mere 63 wins apiece—and 63 wins fewer, oddly enough, than Walter Johnson had all by himself at the same age. The clue that all retired after Ted Williams did means you need the whole lot for a single.

6. In 1922 he notched 22 wins on a 4.07 ERA to become the first 20-game winner since 1900 to allow more than four earned runs a game. Take two bases for him and an RBI if you know his team.

7. In sharp contrast to the above man, this Pittsburgh lefty had a glittering 2.26 ERA in 1915, but only a

6–12 record as the Pirates were blanked eight times in his 18 starts. Tough grand slam even for Iron City historians.

8. He deprived teammate Cy Seymour of the Triple Crown in 1905 when he topped Cy for the home run title by the margin of a single four-bagger. The final irony: he never hit another homer in the majors. Three-run triple.

9. Speaking of homer-crown oddities, only one man in major league history has won his league's four-bagger title and led it that same season in fewest strikeouts. Learning he did it since the advent of the lively ball should make you kick yourself if you don't know him. Two-run double.

10. He had the finest season by a Louisville pitcher during the years the franchise was in the NL when he rang up a 28–15 mark in 1898. Moreover, he did it while fanning just 34 batters in 362 innings—less than one per game. Solo homer.

11. He had a 7–23 record for the woeful Pirates in 1946–47; traded to the powerful Dodgers, he proved what a difference a team can make to a pitcher's stats when he was a dazzling 44–8 during 1951–53. Anyone with both oars in the water will collect an easy double here.

12. Sent to the bullpen in 1971 after clocking a 10–15 record in his last year as a starter, this lefty fireballer and future pitching coach was a snappy 6–0 despite having a 7.04 ERA in 37 games. The clue that he holds a club all-time single-season strikeout record knocks this down to a single. Okay, an RBI for the club.

13. When the Tigers lost at Briggs Stadium on May 2, 1939, by a 22–2 margin, what was the most remarkable thing about the game's box score? Be a shame if these clues aren't enough to net you a two-bagger.

14. As a 19-year-old OB rookie, this fireballer fanned a record 418 batters. Fourteen years later he pitched two no-hitters for the Tigers, missed a third when he surrendered just one hit, a harmless single to the leadoff batter in the game—and yet posted a dismal 5–19 record. Rates just a single, but I'll give two RBIs if you name the leadoff batter who kept him from a record third no-hitter.

SCORING CHART

Potential
Total Bases: 29

Potential
RBIS: 17

At-Bats: 14

Hits:

RBIS:

Total Bases:

9. Great Goats and Victims

1. Aaron victimized him in 1974 when he hit No. 715. Double.

2. His wild pitch in the ninth inning of the fifth game of the 1972 NL League Championship Series gave the underdog Reds the pennant. RBI single.

3. He broke Gus Williams's record for the most strike-outs in a season when he fanned 134 times in 1938. The clue that his younger brother that same season hit 32 homers while whiffing just 21 times should evince the right answer for a single.

4. Who hit the single that would have made him the hero of the 1908 season if only Merkle had touched second base? Two-run double.

5. He set an all-time victim record when the Mets scored nary a run for him in four consecutive games he

started in 1968. Moreover, he gave up only six runs himself in the four games. RBI triple.

6. In his first fall appearance, in 1949, he lost the Series opener 1–0 on Tommy Henrich's ninth-inning homer; he retired with an 0–4 Series record and an 8.59 ERA in five starts. One-run single.

7. The last major leaguer to be banned from the game for attempting to bribe an opponent, he appears in retrospect to have been no more than the unwitting victim of a misguided joke perpetrated by several of his Giants teammates on the last weekend of the 1924 season. RBI double.

8. Eight members of the 1919 White Sox were banned for taking a bribe to throw the 1919 World Series. Who was the only member of the winning Reds later to be banned—and for doing nothing more than taking a college coaching job when he objected to the salary the Reds offered him? Two-run double.

9. He held Leon Culberson's throw a fraction of a second too long, allowing Enos Slaughter to romp all the way home from first base on a single with the run that won the 1946 World Series. Two bases for him, and two RBIs for the guy whose single proved to be the game-winning hit.

10. In 1979 he led the Mariners with 14 wins and 3.77 ERA; the following season something clipped his wings and he collapsed to a 1–16 mark with a 7.28 ERA. RBI single.

11. The leading victim of the "fair-foul" rule change, he spent the 1878 season in the minors after leading the National League with a .429 batting average two years earlier. Which was, of course, 1876, the NL's maiden season, so how can you expect more than a single for knowing its first bat crown winner?

12. Who is the only present Hall of Famer or certain future Hall of Famer to hit below .195 for a full season (400 or more plate appearances)? Double for him; RBI for the year his average tumbled.

13. After serving up Ty Cobb's 4,000th hit in 1927, he spent most of the rest of his career in the minors. But don't feel too sorry for him—he won 307 games there, 28 of them in 1931 when he led all PCL hurlers and pitched the inaugural game for San Francisco in brand-new Seals Stadium, perhaps the finest minor league park ever built. Solo homer.

14. He is the lone pitcher in this century to contrive somehow to lose 20 games for a pennant winner. The clues that he also won 21 and two years later led the AL with 29 victories should aid you to a double.

15. This relief ace's third strike to Tommy Henrich in the 1941 World Series may or may not have been a spitter, but in any case, his receiver, Mickey Owen, became one of the all-time great goats when he missed it. More than enough info there for you to exit with an RBI single.

SCORING CHART

Potential
Total Bases: 27   At-Bats: 15

                                   Hits:

Potential
RBIS: 14   RBIS:

                                   Total Bases:

10. South of the Border

1. The Anglos called him Steve, but in his Cuban home-land he was known as Esteban, and when he per-formed at third base for the Troy Haymakers of the National Association in 1871, he became the first Latin-born player to participate in an American pro-fessional league. Two-run homer.

2. When he netted 27 victories for the 1923 Reds, this Cuban not only set a modern club record, but he became the first Latin-born 20-game winner in the majors. RBI double.

3. The first notable Latino shortstop had an uncle who'd preceded him in the majors by some ten seasons; the uncle finished with the 1949 White Sox, the year before his nephew broke in with the same club. RBI single for the last name of this pair; another RBI for knowing their first names too.

4. This *caballero's* 484 home runs, most of them achieved in the Mexican League, are the most by any player in minor league history. Double.

5. These three brothers were all active in the majors in 1973, making them the first trio of Puerto Rican-born siblings to be on the scene simultaneously; the eldest was still active in 1988. Single.

6. He was the first Latino to win an NL batting title. Single, plus an RBI for the year he became the first.

7. The first outstanding Latino catcher, this Cuban played 17 years in the majors between 1912 and 1932 with five different NL teams and later managed one of them, the Cardinals, briefly, but his real forte may have been his skill as a pitching coach. Two-run double.

8. Name the Cuban catcher who dubbed himself "The Immortal _____" and hit .280 for Cleveland in 1968, his sixth and last season as the Tribe's regular backstopper. Fill in the blank by using the right cues and you've got his last name and an RBI double.

9. The only Latino pitcher to win 25 games twice, he's also the only 25-game winner eligible for a Cy Young Award who never got one. Single.

10. The heaviest Latino contributor to the 1975 AL champs, he had a 14–3 mark that year and a 41–18 career record through 1975; dealt to the Braves the following year, he faded swiftly. Double.

11. He was the first player born in the Dominican Republic to put in ten or more seasons as a regular with the same team. Save you some thought by telling you he came up in the Pirates' chain, finished with the 1972 Reds, played in four World Series, and has a son who's also seen Series action. RBI single.

12. Name the Cuban righty who led the AL in losses a record four consecutive seasons. Last seen in 1970 with a team that bore the same name as the one he started with but was not the same franchise. Work those clues for two bases.

13. What pair of pitching brothers from the Dominican Republic, who died in their homeland 13 days apart in 1977, hold the distinction of being the oldest sibling rookies? The elder was 43 in his frosh season with the 1962 Pirates, the younger a mere 36 with the 1964 Braves. Triple for their last name only; two-run homer if you also correctly hit both their first names.

14. He was the first Puerto Rican-born player to be selected the MVP in the AL. May take you awhile to come up with the answer, but once you do, to his relief you'll agree it only rates a single.

15. He used his brother's passport to get into the U.S. from his native Cuba and thereupon adopted his brother's name throughout a major league career that saw him set an AL rookie record for hits and corner three batting crowns. Single.

SCORING CHART

Potential Total Bases: 27	At-Bats: 15
	Hits:
Potential RBIS: 12	RBIS:
	Total Bases:

11. Minor League Maestros

Told you in the intro that the examination you'd undergo would range far and wide, so you ought to be all set by now to dwell awhile on a few of the great players who appeared only briefly, if that, in the majors, but carved legendary careers in the top minor leagues of their day.

1. In 1906 he led the Texas League with only a .281 average; he retired after the 1929 season with the record for the most games played in the minors (3,282); his one full season in the majors came in 1918 when he served as a backup outfielder for the Red Sox until World Series time, then both his bat and his glove made him the most celebrated player in the land for the next two weeks; come the following spring, however, he was back in the minors to stay. RBI triple.

2. In 1933 he led the PCL in doubles with 63 and had 163 RBIs; thirteen years later he led all Texas League hurlers with a princely 24 wins. The owner of an uneven career at best, this Hawaiian-born pitcher-outfielder nevertheless hit .308 in 30 big league games and was 3–2 as a hurler. Solo homer.

3. He played 2,600 games in the minors, most of them at shortstop. Considered one of the top fielders of his era and perhaps the best ever to play in the PCL, his light stick kept him from finding a home in the majors, where he was a dud, hitting just .223 in 253 games, the bulk of them with the Red Sox in the mid-'20s. Two-run homer.

4. In 1926, while Tony Lazzeri, the first to slug 60 homers in the minors, teamed as a rookie with Babe Ruth, who the following year would be the first to slam 60 in the majors, this A's first sacker hit .192 and gave no intimation that he would one day do what no other slugger before or since has accomplished—hit 60 or more homers in a season twice (63 for Baltimore, IL, in 1930, and 69 for Minneapolis, AA, in 1933). If you don't score an RBI single here, you'd best skip this section, for the minors obviously aren't your dish.

5. In the process of winning back-to-back batting titles in the PCL in 1922–23, this former Boston Braves pitcher-turned-outfielder banged 614 hits over that two-year period, including an OB record 325 in 1923. Two-run double.

6. This lefty-swinging outfielder didn't begin his OB career until 1951 when he was nearly 34; he retired 14 years later with a .352 career batting average, the highest achieved by anyone in OB, majors or minors, since 1941. Learning that the color of his skin accounted for his belated start should help you to an RBI triple.

7. In 1914, twenty years after he'd had a three-game trial in the majors, he retired after playing 2,912 games in the minors, the bulk of them with San Francisco of the PCL. Nothing overly extraordinary about that except that the vast majority of his games were at second base and he was lefthanded—indeed the last lefty infielder of note in OB history. Two-run homer, kid.

8. In 1920 this sweet potato helped demonstrate that the lively ball era had arrived when he became the first catcher ever to hit 40 homers in a season—41 for Wichita of the Western League. For most of the next two seasons he rode the wood as an understudy to Ray Schalk before returning to the minors, where he posted a .315 career average and became the first backstopper to collect over 200 homers. Rough two-run homer for all but minor league aces.

9. He played just one year in the majors and liked it fine until Milwaukee, for whom he'd starred when the AL was still a minor league, dealt him to Washington. Not fond of the East for some reason although he was born there and made his pro debut there, with Pawtucket of the New England League back in the mid-1890s, he played ever after that for teams west of Chicago and starred for years in the AA, PCL, and Western League. In his lone big league sojourn all he did was rap .311 and lead the AL in at-bats. Three-run triple.

10. Cut by the pitcher-rich White Sox in 1919 after a solid rookie season, he found a permanent home for his spitball on the West Coast and won a PCL record 296 games, the last with San Diego in 1936, before becoming a long-time major league coach. One-run double.

11. In 1948, playing for Houma in the Evangeline League, he became the only man in OB history to win a batting Triple Crown and lead his circuit's pitchers in strikeouts and winning percentage that same season. Two-run homer, for this fabled Texan who later played in the Texas League.

12. He had a record nine 20-win seasons in the minors, including six in a row in the PCL (1937–42), but in the majors this Portuguese lefty could never live up to the promise he showed with a 12–5 mark as an A's rookie in 1932. Take three bases and an RBI.

13. Seven years after the above portsider called it quits
    following a 22-win season in 1953 with Stockton in
    the California League, Stockton, by then an Orioles'
    farm club, had a southpaw whiz who fanned 262
    batters in just 170 innings. Unfortunately he walked
    the same number of batters, a problem that would
    plague him throughout his minor league career that
    saw him post a 46–80 record and a 5.59 ERA despite
    whiffing 1,396 men in only 995 innings. Two-bagger
    for this flamethrower of a relatively recent vintage
    that Pat Jordan wrote about so superbly in *The Suit-
    ors of Spring*.

14. He set an all-time OB record in 1919 by hitting safely
    in 69 consecutive games for Wichita of the Western
    League. When it failed to earn him a return ticket to
    the majors, this former Giants outfielder quit four
    years later after hammering .360 for Salt Lake in the
    PCL. Anyone at all knowledgeable about DiMaggio's
    record skein will probably lasso a quick RBI double
    here.

15. He was born in St. Louis and died in Minneapolis,
    which is only fitting. For he began his career as a
    teenage pitcher with the vaunted St. Louis Maroons
    in 1884 and reached his apex when he slugged 45
    homers with Minneapolis of the Western League in
    1895. His home run total, the most in any league
    prior to Babe Ruth's emergence, is tainted in that he
    played in a tiny park where other players also piled
    up astronomical stats for that time. But nothing can
    take away from the fact that he also at one time held
    the record for the most triples in a season, 29 with
    the 1893 St. Louis Browns. Even with all that info
    about this early-day wonder I'll award an RBI single.

SCORING CHART

Potential Total Bases: 42	At-Bats: 15
	Hits:
Potential RBIS: 21	RBIS:
	Total Bases:

12. Super Siblings

1. They were the first pair of brothers each to win 200 or more games in the majors. Snap single.

2. They were the second pair of brothers each to win 200 or more games in the majors. Easier single yet.

3. Gets harder now, but not much. In 1933 the younger sib was 22–7 for Columbus of the AA while his older brother fashioned a 20–18 mark for Columbus's parent club; the next year this pair combined to win a single-season brother-record 49 games for the World Champs. Be a gas if you missed another single because you failed to know not only these famous brothers but their equally famous team.

4. They were the first pair of brothers to face each other as starting pitchers in a major league game. Did it while pitching for the Dodgers and Giants respectively; earlier in their careers they'd both been with the Giants. Take three bases for them and two ribbies for the year they first opposed each other.

5. They would have been the first brothers to oppose each other in a World Series if Cleveland had not fallen short of the pennant by half a game in 1908 and the Pirates had not lost their season finale. Double for nabbing the last name of this pair; homer if you know *both* their first names too.

6. Lee, the younger brother, played on only one pennant winner, but got into a World Series. Jesse, the older, played on three pennant-winning teams after 1900, but was never on a Series participant. Name this pair of brothers whom the fates denied the honor of being the first siblings to play in a modern World Series and take an RBI double.

7. These two brothers starred as outfielders for rival Southern Association teams in 1912; eight years later they became the first siblings to oppose each other in a modern World Series when one held down first base for the World Champs and the other third base for the Series losers. Name both players for an RBI double and take an extra RBI for their teams.

8. They hold both the career and single-season records for the most combined hits by two brothers. Single.

9. These two brothers got short shrift in the majors, but won nine batting titles between them in the minors while hitting a combined .360, far and away the top career sibling average in OB history. Painful to think some of you won't get a triple here.

10. This slugging duo hit 54 homers in 1970, the most by two brothers who played as teammates. RBI single.

11. The only two brothers to hold down the same position for the same team, they shared the Pirates' third base job in 1955. One-run triple.

12. They are the only brothers who collected more career home runs between them than the DiMaggios. Single.

13. One of this trio of brothers is in the Hall of Fame, a second holds the record for the most career home runs by a pitcher, and the third collected 2,876 hits, all in the minor leagues. Mere single, but up to a homer if you know the first names of all three sibs.

14. The only two of seven ball-playing brothers to make the majors, they teamed together briefly in 1888 for Baltimore of the American Association; Mike lost the one game he pitched, but his older sib set an all-time strikeout mark two years earlier as a rookie. Solo homer.

15. Not many Hall of Famers played on the same team in the majors with their brothers. This Brooklyn outfielder became one of the few who did when his backstopping brother joined the club in 1915. Single for knowing only the Famer, but stretched to a triple if you know his brother's first name too.

SCORING CHART

Potential
Total Bases: 34

Potential
RBIS: 10

At-Bats: 15

Hits:

RBIS:

Total Bases:

13. Their Niche Is Secure

1. His 20th-century career record for the most times hit by pitches fell in 1987. For two bases, who's he? An RBI for the man who took his mark from him.

2. His 18 total bases, achieved on four homers and a double, are a one-game major league record. One base for him and an RBI for the park he did it in.

3. The same year that Hoss Radbourn set the major league record with 60 wins, who established the American Association record by winning 52? RBI double for this guy, I'd say.

4. The last names of the only two player-managers in history to win back-to-back World Championships both begin with the same letter. Two hints: it's not Q and one of them's not in the Hall of Fame. Score a triple, but only if you get both. One'll bring you just a sac hit.

5. His 136 walks in 1892 stand as a pre-1901 record; in addition, he once held the season record for the top fielding average by a second baseman. Give a homer here and the clue that he died in 1918 in an insane asylum in the city where he set his bases-on-balls mark.

6. The only two pitchers active exclusively between 1920 and 1960 to toil ten or more full seasons and post career ERAs under 3.00 were both lefties who accomplished most of their success in the NL. Now put your thinking cap on and snatch a homer; single for knowing just one.

7. His 2.86 career ERA is the lowest since expansion among pitchers in over 1,500 innings. Not Ken Schrom and you're not on the A team anymore if you don't collect this RBI single.

8. He holds the records for the longest relief stint in an AL game and being the first umpire to wear glasses to officiate. Double.

9. When he played his 5,342nd consecutive inning in 1985, Cal Ripken toppled the record held by this former Red Sox slugger. Three-bagger.

10. What Dodger lefty resurrected visions of Karl Spooner when he set a record on April 12, 1962, by fanning the first six batters he faced in the majors? Two-run double.

11. His 227 strikeouts in 1911 were the most by any rookie hurler between 1893 and 1955. Double for him; two ribbies for the man who broke his mark.

12. When Tom Seaver netted 289 strikeouts in 1971, whose NL righty record did he break? Even an educated guess should get you in for two here.

13. His 12 shutouts in 1886 gave this cannonballer an all-time southpaw record that still stands in 1990. RBI triple for Pud's pitching mate in the mid-'80s.

14. He holds the AL record for the most shutouts (9) by a lefty in a 154-game season. No, not Chuck Stobbs, but Stobbs broke in with the same team he did. One-run single.

15. He is the lone pitcher since the advent of full-scale free agency in 1977 to produce as many as ten shutouts in a season. One base for him and an RBI for the year he did it.

SCORING CHART

Potential Total Bases: 33	At-Bats: 15
	Hits:
Potential RBIS: 13	RBIS:
	Total Bases:

14. Whatever Happened to …?

Nobody had to ask that question about any of the men you'll meet in this session. For all of them their baseball-playing days were only the beginning.

1. As a teenager he played second fiddle to J. W. Porter, the first two-time American Legion MVP and a much heralded bonus baby in the early '50s. During his major league career he was second to no one, amassing nearly 3,000 hits and becoming the first of his race to go on to a manager's post in the big time. Single.

2. Cap Anson considered this fleet outfielder one of his most valuable players, even though he never hit enough to crack the White Stockings' regular lineup. Traded to Pittsburgh, he swiped 84 bases in 1890, his last season, and then quit to devote himself to evangelism, the field where he achieved eternal fame. Double.

3. Among the first to work his way up through the ranks from player to manager to owner, he found himself head honcho of the most scandal-ridden team in history some 30 years after starring at first base for arguably the most colorful team of the last century. RBI single.

4. A .187 batting average in his third big league season convinced this hot-corner man to forsake baseball for basketball after the 1981 season. He's since starred for an NBA champion. Single.

5. The son of a Baptist minister, he graduated from Brown University the day after he pitched the first perfect game in major league history and went on to become a prominent physician. One-run single.

6. One of the Red Sox mound mainstays in the club's maiden major league season after jumping to the AL from the crosstown Beaneaters, this Welsh-born righty worked over 300 innings and 31 complete games before bidding the Sox adieu and moving on to become a university president. Two-run triple.

7. Last active in the majors in 1890, he hit .311 as a rookie shortstop with Washington and Cincinnati of the American Association in 1884. His chief claim to fame during his playing days was the record 117 errors he made in 1886, but later in life he was elected four times to the Massachusetts legislature. Frankly, if it weren't for that clue about his errors record, this would be a nearly impossible three-run homer.

8. A baseball injury may have been a blessing in disguise for him. The holder of the Eastern League season home run record, he quit the game after ripping .341 as an outfielder for Toronto of the IL in 1931 and went on to become a Hall of Fame kicker and running back in the NFL. RBI double.

9. Among the few great players to exit from baseball while still at the peak of his game, he returned to his West Coast home grounds and soon amassed a fortune as a real estate baron in the San Francisco Bay area. Departed at 28 with a .330 career average, all of it compiled in the 1890s with Chicago. Two-run double.

10. This pair ended the 1940s as sub infielders who played behind Gil Hodges and Joe Gordon respectively; by the conclusion of the following decade each was the star of a popular TV show. They're worth one base apiece, and the TV programs they headed are going for an RBI apiece.

11. For many years a noted New York sportswriter, he died in 1925 of pneumonia contracted while covering a Giants game on an inclement day. In his last effort as a major league manager, 41 years earlier, he led the Cincinnati Unions to an amazing 36 victories in the 43 games he skippered them from his position at second base. Overhand pitching finished him soon thereafter—he hit .153 in the NL two years later—but you should be able to take this sidearm sling deep for a homer.

12. He tried and failed to crack the regular Yankees outfield just prior to the arrival of Babe Ruth, but was eminently successful at leading the team that during the next two decades would be the Yankees of pro football. RBI single—and another easy one for all-around sports fans.

13. He was 4–26 in his only big league campaign—1876 with the last-place Cincinnati Red Stockings in the fledgling National League. It's by far the worst record of any hurler who pitched just one season in the majors, but save the pity for yourself if you don't know him. Upon leaving the game, he founded a prosperous electrotype business and became a crack tennis player, so good that he was still winning tournaments in the 1930s after he'd celebrated his 80th birthday. Three-run homer.

14. Lots of players have moved upstairs to the broadcast booth after retiring. But this former catcher is one of the few dexterous enough to rap about other sports as well as baseball and was the only former big leaguer to appear in living rooms everywhere during the 1988 Winter Olympics. Single.

15. He led the AL in pinch hits as a rookie third sacker for the Yankees, quit the game seven years later for medicine, and became in the course of time the first former player to leave the game for another career and then return as the prexy of a major league. Single.

SCORING CHART

Potential
Total Bases: 30

Potential
RBIS: 17

At-Bats:15

Hits:

RBIS:

Total Bases:

June

Leader of the Pack

In 1941, Ted Williams hit .406 for the Red Sox and Nashville first baseman Les Fleming rapped .414 to top the Southern Association. Since then no player in either the majors or the high minors has cracked the .400 barrier. Indeed, precious few have even come close to doing it. In the majors there have been only three serious challenges to the magic figure in the past 49 seasons.

One occurred in 1957 when Williams hit .388, another in 1980 when George Brett flirted with the .400 mark for much of the season before finishing at .390. But Williams, due to age, and Brett, owing to injuries, both sat out a lot of games and thus collected only 420 and 449 at-bats respectively. The third serious challenger, in contrast, had 616 at-bats. On that count alone his season is the best of the three; nobody will dispute that the more at-bats a player collects, the harder it is for him to maintain an astronomical average.

But weighing against our man's performance—on initial glance at least—is the fact that it came in an expansion year. Typically, there are always a welter of super hitting and slugging feats in a season when expansion occurs, and especially in the league that is expanding. On closer inspection, however, it turns out that such wasn't the case when our man made his run at the .400 mark. Actually, the only stats that year that could be called at all exceptional were his own, and they were not merely exceptional—they were mammoth.

First off, he outhit the average player in his league by 122 points, the widest differential between a leader and the rest of the pack since expansion and the second widest differential since 1941. But the huge disparity between what he hit and what the pack hit is only the frosting on the cake. Our man also had 239 hits, 128 runs, 100 RBIs, 38 doubles, 16 triples, 14 homers, and 23 stolen bases to make him the only player since World War II to collect over 220 hits, be in triple digits in runs and RBIs, and double digits in everything else.

For a bingle, who are we talking about here? Credit an extra base for knowing the year he soared—and two RBIs for knowing his exact average that year.

15. Team Teasers

1. This team won one fewer game on the road (54) than the A's, the seventh-place team in its league that year, won at home and away combined. Single for the team; RBI for the year it happened; a second RBI for knowing the cellar-dweller that won *nine* fewer games all told than our heroes won on foreign turf.

2. They unloaded a future home run king for shortstop Frank Duffy one season. Before the year was out, they swapped Duffy and a future 300-game winner for a sore-armed lefty with personal problems who had only 19 wins left in his wing. Triple if you know the whole bundle—the team, the year it was so generous, the home run leader, and the two pitchers. Down to a single if you stumble on one or more of the players, and a goose egg without the right team and year.

3. What Hall of Famer in 1933 ended the Yankees' record of 308 consecutive games without being shut out? Single for him; RBI for getting his team too.

4. How about another single for the only team that's had an MVP winner on three different occasions when it finished in the second division? And an RBI in your column if you know all three players who shone in otherwise lackluster company.

5. They won three consecutive pennants without having a 20-game winner. Hint: they were the first club

to win an NL flag lacking a 20-game winner. Single, plus an RBI for the years it happened.

6. They played in the last wood park in the majors. Single for the team; up to a double if you know the year they quit playing in a firetrap; and two RBIs for the name of it.

7. They were the last major league team to play in a park that seated fewer than 30,000. Single for the team and the name of its old park; an RBI for the year the club moved to more commodious digs.

8. What is the only park that was called home by three different major league teams in this century? To gain an RBI single you need the park and all three teams.

9. They were the last of the 16 original franchises to host an All-Star game; to add insult, the contest was rained out after the fifth inning. Double for the team; an RBI apiece for the rain-out year and the park the team occupied.

10. In 1983 they not only won the American Association flag, but became the first team in minor league history to draw over 1,000,000 fans. RBI single.

11. The Yankees have retired the uniform numbers of 11 players. The Tigers, in contrast, have never retired the uniform number of their greatest star. For a deuce, who is he and why haven't the Bengals granted him this distinction?

12. They're the only one of the 16 original major league franchises that hasn't had a 25-game winner since 1921. Double for the team; knowing its last 25-game winner rates two RBIs.

13. They're the lone team since 1945 to miss winning a flag despite having a pitcher who won 27 or more games—moreover, it happened twice! Single for the team; two RBIs for knowing both pitchers.

14. The NL began in 1876 as an eight-club circuit. For the next two seasons it was forced to limp along with only six teams when two clubs refused to complete their final western road trips in 1876, compelling the fledging league to expel them in a show of authority. Take a double if you know the two teams whose departure nearly sunk the NL in its infancy.

15. In 1953, their last season playing in the city that had been their domicile since 1902, they lost a record 20 straight home games. Too many good clues for this to sell for any more than an RBI single.

16. Excepting the strike-shortened 1981 season, only once has a team won a pennant without a pitcher who had at least 15 victories. Fact is, this club had nobody who won more than 11. What's the catch? None, my man. You simply weren't paying attention when it happened. Single for the team; RBI for the year.

SCORING CHART

Potential Total Bases: 23	At-Bats: 16
	Hits:
Potential RBIS: 18	RBIS:
	Total Bases:

16. Now Batting For ...

Those three words alone could automatically bring a chill to fans who knew that one of the men we'll meet in this session was lurking on tap in the enemy dugout.

1. He hit the first pinch homer in Series history. Happened in the 44th World Series in this century. RBI double.

2. He garnered the first pinch hit in Series history. Could give a million clues, but two will have to suffice. It was his last career pinch hit and his victim was Three Finger Brown. Two-run homer.

3. His record for having at least one pinch hit in every season of an 18-year career was broken in 1980, 13 years after he retired, when Manny Mota did it for a 19th straight season. RBI single.

4. The game's first great pinch hitter, this catcher was averaging .453 in pinch roles until he went 1-for-11 for the 1904 Red Sox; at the time he held the record for the most pinch blows in a season (8), set with Washington in 1897. Two-run double for the AA's top slugger in its last year as a major circuit.

5. He holds the current mark for the most pinch hits in a season (25). Single.

6. In 1943 this Red Sox player-manager and future Hall of Famer became the first to hit pinch homers in both halves of a doubleheader. Double.

7. His 17 pinch blows for the Tigers in 1920 set both a new AL and a new rookie record. Learning that in 1925 he hit .345 as the A's regular third sacker could help you score a two-run homer here.

8. The Giants made him a regular after he rapped .425 (17-for-40) as a pinch hitter in 1986. Single.

9. He set a new record when he homered in three consecutive pinch-hit plate appearances in 1979. What, you missed it? Well, here's a big help. His father had two pinch hits while serving as the Reds backup catcher in 1945. Two-bagger.

10. His 20 pinch bingles in 1913 for the Phillies set a new major league record that stood until 1932. Two-run double.

11. Well, natch, now I'm going to ask you whose 22 pinch safeties in 1932 set a new major league mark. Two years later he had 102 RBIs and hit .332 as the Dodgers first sacker. RBI double.

12. Among players presently in the Hall of Fame who had a minimum of 100 pinch at-bats during their careers, his .322 pinch-hitting average heads the list. Unless you happen to know this, it'll probably take a pretty lucky guess to snag an RBI single here.

13. In 1933 this frosh receiver went 1-for-31 as a pinch hitter for the Dodgers; at that he was more success-ful than the Braves backstopper who was 0-for-31 in pinch roles in 1924. The Dodgers rookie never played in the majors again, but the Boston catcher ironically had an outstanding .337 average as a pinch hitter excluding that one disastrous season. Name either man for a two-run double. Grand slam homer for both.

14. Name the Cardinals pitcher and older brother of the catcher for the 1920 World Champs who in 1902 hit the first pinch grand slam homer in major league history. Two-run homer.

15. These two Browns outfielders set a teammate record in 1936 when they collected 38 pinch hits between them. Neither ever played in the majors again and the top man, the first in AL history to post 20 pinch raps in a season, further set the all-time pinch-hit record (since tied by Chris Chambliss) for a player in his final campaign. Name both for a wicked three-run homer; double for knowing only the man who had 20. Can't believe anybody'd know the other guy and not him, so I feel safe awarding a two-run homer in the event someone out there does.

SCORING CHART

Potential Total Bases: 36	At-Bats: 15
	Hits:
Potential RBIS: 21	RBIS:
	Total Bases:

17. Moments to Remember

1. He won the MVP Award when he hit .273 and led the AL in doubles, triples, and runs. He never again hit .250—two years later, in fact, he stroked a mere .200 in 100 games. A breeze of a double for anybody over thirty.

2. This Hall of Famer played center field for Cleveland on Opening Day in 1946. Two years later he won 20 games and threw a no-hitter. Two-run single.

3. After leading the Southern Association with a .354 average, the following year he became the lone man ever to hit .400 in his first full major league season. Only the fact that it happened a while back makes this a double.

4. His suit against baseball when the Cards tried to trade him against his wishes after the 1969 season helped open the floodgates for free agency. Want an RBI to go with this easy single? Just name the only team he subsequently played for.

5. He played in the first National Association game in 1871, the first National League game in 1876, and in 1884 was the lone Boston batter Charlie Sweeney failed to whiff in his record 19-K game. Solo homer.

6. His first full season as player-manager saw his batting average dip 86 points— but he led his club to the first modern-era pennant in a city that hadn't had a winner since 1888. Single, plus an RBI for the year he did it.

7. This 5'4" mighty mite debuted in a big way for Cincinnati of the AA in 1888, winning his first eight games en route to a 27-victory season before losing 3–1 to Brooklyn on June 1. Put a three-run homer on the board.

8. After Tommy Tucker led the AA in batting in 1889, some 67 years elapsed before another switch hitter copped a major league bat crown. For a single, who broke the ice?

9. He narrowly missed becoming the first switch hitter in this century to win a bat title when he lost out to Carl Furillo by two points in 1953. Two-bagger.

10. After a super 29–8 season in 1905 with Columbus of the American Association, he was acquired by the dismal Braves and saw his fortunes almost exactly reverse when he posted an 8–26 record in 1906 and led the NL in losses. Even I will admit this is a pretty rough three-run homer.

11. In 1955 he had a 14–9 record and a 2.83 ERA to become the first ERA leader to pitch for a last-place team. Score one for him and an RBI for the team.

12. In his first pro year this 18-year-old righthander was 21–8 for Newark in the Ohio State League; seven years later he became the St. Louis Browns' last 20-game winner—and with a cellar dweller yet. Snap up a run-scoring double.

13. On July 7, 1884, he became the second hurler in major league history to fan 19 men in a game and ought to have been the first to whiff 20—he lost a K

when his catcher, Bill Krieg, missed a third strike, allowing a batter to reach first base safely (the scoring rules at the time didn't credit a strikeout unless the hitter was retired). Knowing he lost something far more vital in his youth—his left forearm—should make this a cush three-bagger.

14. In 1958 this Phillie became the last batsman to lead either major league in strikeouts with fewer than 100 when he whiffed a mere 95 times. For those into the game's evolution this will make a neat homer.

15. Once upon a time he led the majors in wins while pitching for a last-place team. He's the only pitcher who ever accomplished this feat, and your only clue is that his club brought up the rear in its division, not the entire league. RBI single.

SCORING CHART

Potential
Total Bases: 33

Potential
RBIS: 15

At-Bats: 15

Hits:

RBIS:

Total Bases:

18. Glorious Glovemen

1. His 16 Gold Gloves are the most won by any player other than a pitcher. Single.

2. He was the first backstopper to catch 150 or more games during a season in which he collected fewer assists than he scored runs. Huh? Well, think about it for a minute. Obviously a workhorse, obviously provided some offensive contribution—and perhaps

not so obviously, he played at a time when catchers began nailing a lesser percentage of would-be base thieves. Take three bases.

3. He is the only player in history who twice had a perfect 1.000 FA for a season in which he played 130 or more games in the field. Quite recent history. Double.

4. He leads all pitchers in career putouts. Not tough at all, especially if you know that the top all-time leaders are all from our era. One-run single.

5. He holds the single-season record for the most assists by a first baseman. And at one time he held both the AL and the NL marks. That and my helpful hint that it isn't Dick Stuart makes this just a single.

6. Excluding catchers, he is the only career leader in total chances at his position who's not in the Hall of Fame. So why not? you ask. Good question. Two-bagger.

7. His 512 putouts in 1977 set an AL single-season record for outfielders. RBI double, on the gamble that a fair number of you weren't paying attention that year.

8. To break the string of relatively easy questions, here's a real zinger. For a two-run homer, name the lone first sacker to make four errors in a game twice. Why only a two-run shot? Because I'm going to add that he did it both times in 1904 and that he also set a record that season for being the youngest regular in NL history.

9. His 641 assists in 1927 are by far the most ever by a second baseman. Deservedly a Hall of Famer, and all you deserve for knowing him is a single.

10. So now spew forth the name of the second baseman—and the only infielder active prior to 1900—who ranks among the top ten at his position in most single-season assists. The huge clue that he was responsible for a team being given the nickname it still possesses makes this only a double, plus an RBI for the nickname.

11. In 1907 this frail-hitting pastureman led all AL out-fielders with a .990 FA while making just 182 put-outs, a record low for gardeners in 150 or more games. Even with the clue that he was with the Hitless Wonders in 1906, you're a dark-horse to homer here.

12. Now for the above man's antithesis. What Cardinal in 1928 set an all-time record for outfielders when he had 566 putouts and handled a modern-record 3.7 chances per game? Should hit this for a double.

13. This Hall of Famer was death on bunts. In 1907 he broke Will White's ancient record for pitchers when he nabbed 227 assists. A year later he had 190. No other pitcher before or since White has ever col-lected more than 178, and you're a heavy favorite to collect an RBI single.

14. Jimmy Piersall retired in 1967 with a .990 career FA, breaking the career record for outfielders active ten or more seasons that was formerly held by what one-time slugging champ with a .989 FA? There's a double afoot here, Watson.

15. Hey, enough of all these great glovemen, right? How about some that weren't so terrific? Sure, just mur-mur the name of the most recent regular to post a season FA below .900 and you've got another RBI double. Easily when I add that I do mean recent, like 1978, and that if you're just guessing, you've been reduced to a single choice.

SCORING CHART

Potential Total Bases: 30	At-Bats: 15
	Hits:
Potential RBIS: 8	RBIS:
	Total Bases:

19. Like Father Like Son

1. He is the only Hall of Famer who began as a pitcher to father a son who had more career wins than he did in the majors. Furthermore, he had another son whose hit won a pennant, something none of his many feats ever brought him. Nail him and both his offspring for a single.

2. In 1946 this lefty burned the Cards when he jumped to the Mexican League after zipping off to a 6–0 start; forty years later his son skippered a team that burned the rest of the NL West. RBI single.

3. Senior was the starting pitcher for the Philadelphia A's in their famous 18–17 game with Cleveland in 1932; Junior threw a shutout at age 18 in his debut with the Kansas City A's 29 years later. RBI double.

4. He played some 18 years in the minors before appearing in four games with the Phillies in 1944. His son never made the majors at all, but has played for and coached several NBA championship teams. Neat change-of-pace bingle for all-around sports fans; full credit even if you don't know the father.

5. His 34 homers in 1987, his soph season, were 32 more than his father, also an outfielder, hit in a nine-year career. RBI single.

6. The first black player to father a son who played in the majors, he sired two, no less. Name all three men for a homer; single if you merely know the family name.

7. In 1910 he was the Braves regular catcher; 39 years later his son led the Browns in homers with the third highest total in the AL. Be a peach of a three-bagger if you know both.

8. He hit .291 and had 27 doubles for Cleveland in 1951; his son, in 1982, set the NL record for the most doubles by a catcher. Single.

9. In 1,027 games this catcher posted a .249 career batting average and a mere .283 slugging average; in 1,192 games his son, a shortstop-outfielder, had a paltry .245 career batting average but a .411 slugging average. RBI single.

10. The Gordy Howe of baseball, in 1946 this former A's first sacker at age 51 played in the same infield with his son for Moultrie of the Georgia-Florida League. The son never did much, but the old man still holds the Southern Association single-season home run record. RBI triple.

11. The first father and son combo who each played at least ten seasons in the majors, the old man batted .214 for the Hitless Wonders and went 0-for-21 in the 1906 World Series; his son, also a catcher, hit .351 for Cleveland in 1935. Double.

12. Barred from OB for allegedly throwing games after he hit .370 for Seattle of the PCL in 1920, this ex-A's outfielder sired a son who played for the only major league team other than the Yankees that Casey Stengel managed to a better-than-.500 finish. Tough but intriguing two-run homer, so go for it.

13. He was the first to play in the majors for a team managed by his old man. Sorry, but you gotta get his first name to score an RBI double; sac hit if you only know his dad.

14. When his son debuted with the Pirates in 1986, only five years after he left the majors, this pair became one of the few father-son combos to play in the same decade. Single.

15. They hold the record for the most combined career hits by a father-son combo. Or trio for that matter. Enough there to score another single.

SCORING CHART

Potential Total Bases: 28	At-Bats: 15
	Hits:
Potential RBIS: 9	RBIS:
	Total Bases:

20. World War II Wrinkles

We're talking now specifically about the three years (1943–45) when the game was major league in name only while many of its stars were in the armed services. So most historians contend. Tell you right up front, though, that I don't wholly agree, and some of the questions in this session spring from observations about those inimitably weird seasons that may key you, too, to reassess what went on in them.

1. After leading the NL in home runs in 1942, he hit all of .234 in 1943, the first year of wartime baseball. Only 34 at the time, he made the Hall of Fame eight years later. Can't duck that embarrassingly low BA if you want an RBI single.

2. Of the players who lost at least three full seasons to WWII and were among the top five hitters in their league in their last season prior to a service interruption, only one—.331 in 1942 and .335 in 1946—posted a higher batting average upon his return. Two-run double.

3. His 22 home runs led the AL in 1944, the year the rubber shortage really started to make itself felt. Considered strictly a wartime ball player but, hey, he hit .311 for the Phils in 1941. Three-bagger.

4. Heavily battered as a starter for the A's, he was acquired by the Browns in 1941 and set an all-time Brownie save record three years later when he notched 12 for the flag winners. Cast deep into your memory bank and score a homer.

5. His 63 wins between 1943–45 led all wartime hurlers. Shouldn't have to cast nearly as deep to hook this fish. RBI double.

6. Traded against his will to the Dodgers, this Hall of Famer led the NL in steals and runs in 1943, then quit the game rather than play for Durocher, and refused to return until 1947, when Leo was suspended for the season. One-run single.

7. The worst hitting team in the majors just prior to 1943, the Phils scored a post-1920-low 394 runs in 1942. During the war years nothing changed. The Phils, in fact, had just one .300 hitter—he rapped .300 on the nose in 1945. For a two-run homer name this former Cleveland sandlot star who finished his career in Lakefront Stadium.

8. He was the lone NL'er to swipe 20 or more bases twice during the war. Also led the NL in triples in 1944 and the Pirates in homers in 1945. RBI triple.

9. Plagued by migraine headaches, this slugging first sacker, though only 28, was forced to quit in 1941. A comeback attempt in 1944 with the White Sox saw him hit just .241, but lead the club in both homers and RBIs with totals that were about half of what he averaged in his prime. Two-bagger.

10. This shortstop had 917 at-bats for the wartime A's and fanned just 28 times, including but nine in 1945, a low for AL regulars. Knowing that he had no career homers and only 27 extra-base hits could help you nail this keystoner who specialized in making contact albeit with a feather. Three-run homer.

11. He was the only regular (300+ at bats) on the draft-riddled 1943 World Champs to hit .280 or better. A rookie at the time, he later played regularly for the 1943 Series losers. Two-run double.

12. En route to winning a batting title and a slugging crown—with the lowest slugging average since 1920 by a leader—he collected 22 triples, the most by anyone between 1931 and 1948. RBI single.

SCORING CHART

Potential Total Bases: 27	At-Bats: 12
	Hits:
Potential RBIS: 14	RBIS:
	Total Bases:

21. Their Niche Is Secure

1. After his first six seasons he had a 36–40 record; over his next six seasons he went 129–47 and led the NL in ERA a record five straight times. Single.

2. In 1954 this righthander posted a 3–21 record, the worst in this century for a 20-game loser; two years later, at the season's close, he was the toast of baseball. Hard to imagine anybody'd need any more clues than that to rack up a double.

3. He set an all-time record when he began his career with ten consecutive 20-win seasons. Slap this one for an RBI single, kid, or be forever sorry.

4. After six seasons this shortstop had a .305 career average, had twice topped 200 hits, and had become the first ever to rap 100 hits in a season from each side of the plate. He completed the 1989 season with a .275 career average. Single.

5. He is the only umpire in major league history to be banned from baseball for rigging games in which he officiated. Triple for him; two ribbies for the year his chicanery set him down.

6. He holds the all-time OB single-season record in a major offensive department with a stat higher than the amount he achieved in the same department in *any other two seasons combined* during his nine-year major league career. Learning that 27 was his total in this department in his next two best seasons combined and that it's exactly three-quarters of what he got in his top year makes your job only about one-quarter as hard. Which explains why you only are up for a single with an RBI if you know the year he wowed the entire baseball world.

7. He set a record for shortstops in 1949 when he banged 159 RBIs. RBI double.

8. He is the only shortstop to collect more than 40 home runs in a season. Single.

9. His 213 hits in 1986 are the most in major league history by a shortstop. This feat, rather strangely,

got so little notice that I have to award two bases here.

10. He led his league in complete games a record nine times. If you're only guessing here, a double says you'll guess the wrong moundsman.

11. He is the lone pitcher to cop as many as four Cy Young Awards. If you're only guessing here, you're a solid bet to hit about .045 in this book. Single.

12. In 1969 he was the only player among the top ten in career runs who hadn't made either 3,000 hits or 200 homers. He's since fallen out of the top ten, but his reputation for being a great run-maker without being either a slugger or an extraordinarily prolific hit producer hasn't diminished one iota. A savvy guess and you're in with a triple.

13. Apart from Babe Ruth, only two Hall of Famers who played ten or more seasons have retired with career slugging averages that were nearly double their career batting averages. Both their last names begin with the same letter, and you need 'em both to obtain an RBI double. Sac hit for just one.

14. He was the last man to retire with a career slugging average above .560. Just a single.

15. In 1920, the first year the lively ball had a pervasive impact on the game, Babe Ruth had a record .847 slugging average, a figure nearly double that of the player who led the NL in slugging the previous year. Go out on a high note by notching a triple for naming the Dodger whose .436 mark topped the senior circuit in 1919.

SCORING CHART

Potential
Total Bases: 27

At-Bats: 15

Hits:

Potential
RBIS: 6

RBIS:

Total Bases:

July

Rapid Robert's Redux

Bob Feller returned from the navy to the Indians late in the 1945 season and immediately demonstrated that he still had the blazing fastball that prior to the war had registered the then-existing single-game strikeout record. The following year he set his sights on Rube Waddell's modern single-season strikeout mark of 343, set in 1904. By the end of the 1946 campaign, after fanning 348 hitters, Feller had seemingly achieved his goal. But then the fun began. When box scores of the games Waddell had pitched in 1904 were reexamined, discrepancies were revealed in ten of them, making it appear that Waddell had really collected 349 strikeouts. Earl Hilligan, the chief of the American League's service bureau, at first refused to accept the new total, saying, "It would be unfair to change the record at this late date without absolutely unchallengeable evidence." That kind of evidence never emerged, but the American League nevertheless recanted and credited Waddell with six additional strikeouts in 1904.

As a result, Feller was the record-holder for a brief while only and at that never officially. But in any event, his 348 K's represent the most by a pitcher in either major league between 1904 and 1965. Many analysts feel that his performance that year was the most awesome single-season strikeout feat in history with the possible exception of Waddell's in 1904. It was so awesome that it obscured the fact that another American Leaguer in 1946 collected 275 strikeouts, the *second* highest total registered by any junior loop hurler between 1913 and 1964.

If you're thinking that 1946 for some reason must have been a particularly rich year for strikeouts, it wasn't. It was an outstanding year for the man who had 275—and a great one for Feller—but barely an average year for every other pitcher. The National League, as an example, was led by Johnny Schmitz with only 135 K's, not even half as many as the AL runner-up amassed.

For a two-bagger, name the man who trailed Rapid Robert in the 1946 race for K honors while fanning the most men in a 154-game season of any lefty in AL history save for Waddell.

22. Moments to Remember

1. In 1985 he became the first player since George Kell to collect 100 or more RBIs and fewer than ten home runs. Single, and yes, an RBI for the year Kell did it.

2. His 240 hits in 1986 were the most by anyone in the AL since _____ had _____ in _____. Single for the 240-man and an RBI for each blank correctly filled in. Three runs on a single? Hey, it's been done.

3. This Hall of Famer's loss to lowly Pittsburgh on October 5, 1889, cost Boston the NL flag in the first pennant race in major league history decided on the final day of the season. Single for the Famer; RBI for the team that won the flag.

4. Since Maris clocked 61 homers in 1961, only two players have topped the 50 mark. Single for both; but each of the years they did it rates a ribby.

5. Knowing that Tigers pinch hitter Johnny Bassler was the last man he faced should be all you need to collect a double for knowing the only pitcher prior to Don Larsen to hurl a perfect game since the advent of the lively ball.

6. A bit quixotic but still memorable. Grab a homer for knowing the only man to be a league leader in a batting, pitching, or fielding department who had either a first or last name beginning with the letter X.

7. He was the last lefthanded hitter to post a season average of over .420. Double for the player; three ribbies if you know the year he did it.

8. Given a brief trial by the Yankees in 1938, he lost his first big league decision. A year later he reeled off 12 straight wins for the Bombers before suffering his second defeat. Three bases for this fireballer.

9. Surely you'll know the last NL'er to hit .330 or better four years in a row if I announce that he did it in an era when the AL had only one .330+ average during that span. Going for a double.

10. After setting a new pro record when he clubbed 71 doubles for Toledo in 1900 and led the Interstate League with a .360 mark, he cracked a double in the AL's inaugural game as a major circuit the following year to make him the first AL'er to register an extra-base hit. The next day he hit the first AL home run. By 1903, despite two fine seasons up top, he was back in the minors with Shreveport of the Southern Association, where he hit .331. Take a home run yourself for this shooting star whose four-base blow is remembered best in Cleveland.

11. In 1949 this Giants lefty was the first hurler in history to lead his loop in ERA with a losing record; he finished 11–14 with a 2.50 ERA. Double.

12. Want a grand slam? It's yours for the name of the pitcher who hurled the opening game for the St. Louis Maroons on April 20, 1884, and launched their all-time-record 20 consecutive wins to start the season. I'll toss in that the game went only six innings before rain ended it, and our man went only half a season before an ulcerated foot shelved him permanently.

13. A 20-game winner with the NL's top winning percentage in 1933, this Braves righty plummeted two

years later to 25 losses and the NL's worst winning percentage, an abysmal .138. Two-run triple.

14. He is the only slugger who holds the season home run record for two different franchises. RBI single.

15. Close with another RBI single by naming the only hurler to pitch a perfect game on the closing day of the season.

SCORING CHART

Potential Total Bases: 32	At-Bats: 15
	Hits:
Potential RBIS: 19	RBIS:
	Total Bases:

23. North of the Border

Only fair, wouldn't you say, after devoting thought to the many Latino and Chicano contributors that we give some time to our neighbors from the north.

1. Born in Melville, Saskatchewan, he broke in with the Astros in 1977 and finished the 1989 season with the best career fielding average in history by an outfielder. Single.

2. Easily the winningest pitcher born north of the border, he departed in 1983 with 284 victories. Single.

3. You really think it's going to stay that simple? How about naming the first Canadian-born player to make his mark in the majors? He played regularly at first base for three different teams from 1879–88, achieving his apex in 1885 when he hit .302 for Brooklyn of the AA. Three-run homer.

4. This French-speaking first sacker ripped pitchers in the Western Canadian League for a .377 mark with Moose Jaw in 1911, led the AL in slugging average four years later, and then dropped down to the PCL for several years before resurfacing in the NL, where he starred until 1927 after leading the senior loop in homers in 1924. Treat yourself to an RBI double.

5. A Harvard grad from Nova Scotia, he first hit the majors with Cincinnati in 1880 and lasted until 1891. Never much of a hitter, he was an outstanding middle infielder and had his best years with Pittsburgh, where he performed behind Hall of Famer Pud Galvin. Two-run homer.

6. One of the top French-Canadian players of all time, he spent the early '30s shuttling back and forth between the majors and the high minors until he landed in Montreal, where he had four fine seasons. Later a Southern Association leader in homers and RBIs, he had his finest hour in 1931 when he led the American Association with a loop-record .419 average, albeit in only 93 games. Triple.

7. The pride of Drumheller, Alberta, this outfielder set a new world record in 1957 when he threw a baseball 445' 10"—a whole lot farther than he ever hit one in earlier trials with the Phillies. Two-run double.

8. This Ontario-born catcher was a long way from home in 1902 when he hit eight homers in eight at-bats for Corsicana in a Texas League game; three years later he came back north, to Cleveland, where he became the Naps regular catcher and was credited by some historians with being the first backstopper to wear shin protectors. RBI double.

9. The first brother act sent to us by Canada, John, the younger half, was a regular only one of his eight seasons, but his older sibling played short on the first team to win a World Series and later succeeded

Harry Wright as the manager of the Phillies. Oldies experts will lap up an easy three-bagger.

10. He returned to his London, Ontario, home after catching in the majors for 14 seasons, most of them with the Pirates, and died there in 1967 when he was 86. Shouldn't need to know more than that he was a fine defensive backstopper and the first to catch 150 games in a season. Double.

11. Yet another famous-first contributor who came to us from Canada was this Cleveland outfielder and pinch hitter deluxe who became the first former player to move upstairs to the radio booth, where he served the Tribe as a broadcaster for over 30 years. Can't in good conscience give more than an RBI single here.

12. Only a select elite will be sharp enough to recall the Canadian-born outfielder who played part-time with the Giants during WWII before sliding back to the Western International League, where he starred for years with Vancouver. Four-run homer.

13. Another very rugged question, I'll admit, but many would find me remiss if I didn't ask who was the first player to win a batting title in a league under the aegis of Organized Baseball while wearing a Montreal or Toronto uniform. Rates as another grand slam even if I add the footnote that he also did some pitching and reputedly once killed a batter with a beanball in a minor league game.

SCORING CHART

Potential Total Bases: 33	At-Bats: 13
	Hits:
Potential RBIS: 18	RBIS:
	Total Bases:

24. Super Siblings

1. The largest collection of brothers ever to play in the majors, no two of the five ever played as regulars at the same time for the same team, but a pair of them did play together with Minneapolis of the AA in 1912. Single for the family name; two-run homer for the pair who were 1912 teammates.

2. They were the first brother battery act to work together for a full game in the AL. Easy homer for those who had Bosox season tickets in '29.

3. They were the first brothers who both had 20-win seasons in the majors. The clue that they refused to pitch against each other may aid some to a two-bagger.

4. They're the only pair of pitching brothers who both threw a no-hitter in the majors. One base for them, and each of the two years they first did it is worth an RBI.

5. On September 29, 1986, they became the first siblings in major league history to oppose each other as rookie starting pitchers. Shouldn't need more than that to tuck away an RBI single.

6. The pitching-short 1884 Chicago White Stockings employed the brother of their ace boxman in one game and then cut him after he threw five wild pitches and gave up 16 hits. The last name alone rates a three-bagger; zap this pair's first names, too, and you're good for a three-run homer.

7. This pair of brothers were teammates in the club that lost the 1959 NL pennant playoff series to the Dodgers; the elder played first base while the younger was back of the plate. Two-bagger.

8. They hold the record for the most career hits by a trio of brothers. Many will stumble over the wrong trio trying for this RBI single.

9. The Recciuses were the first twins to play in the majors, the Hunters were probably the most obscure, and the O'Briens the most famous. But the most talented twins may well have been this outfield pair who starred in the minors from 1922–34 with only one of them ever seeing major league action and at that for just a few games. Teammates for only one season, their first, with Bristol of the Appalachian League, they'll be an easy homer for experts.

10. The mound half of this brother act holds the record for the most consecutive games hitting a home run as a starting pitcher; the other half is a cinch to one day make the Hall of Fame. Single.

11. In 1941 two members of this trio of brothers had 100+ RBIs, and the third was among the stolen-base leaders in his league. Need the first names of all three to score a single here.

12. He's the only member of the 1927 Yankees with a .300+ career average and 1500+ hits who isn't in the Hall of Fame; his brother is the only member of the Giants' powerhouse team earlier in the decade with the same credentials who isn't in the Hall of Fame. Need the first names of both for an RBI single; sac hit if you nab only one.

13. In 1927 these two brothers had over 1,000 combined at-bats and hit a combined .306. Between them, however, they managed just one home run. The clues that they were teammates for ten years in the 1920s and that one's in the Hall of Fame ought to make this a sure two-bagger.

14. They opposed each other in the 1964 World Series. Want more? They played the same position. Still more? Hey, this is a quiz, not a giveaway. Single.

15. The elder had 100+ RBIs in three different seasons with three different teams; the younger led the White Sox in homers and RBIs in 1973. Want more? Okay, combined they have the same number of career home runs as the '64 Series sibs. Single.

SCORING CHART

Potential	At-Bats: 15
Total Bases: 30	
	Hits:
Potential	
RBIS: 12	RBIS:
	Total Bases:

25. Great Goats and Victims

1. He became an all-time victim instead of an instant hero when his line shot with two men on base was speared by Bobby Richardson to end the 1962 World Series. RBI single.

2. His 10–19 record for the 1938 Cubs is far and away the worst mark by a pitcher involved in 25 or more decisions for a flag-winner. After being told he narrowly missed becoming the first pitcher in history to collect 200 victories without ever having a 20-win season, you surely ought to get an RBI double.

3. In 1968 he was second in the AL in strikeouts and had a 3.85-ERA—not a bad season you'll think, until you discover his 3.85 ERA was the worst in the AL that year by a pitcher in enough innings to be an ERA qualifier. All of a sudden this question became a lot more interesting, didn't it? One-run double.

4. Pirates first sacker Bob Robertson hit .193 in 1972 for the defending World Champs. What first sacker hit .171 for the defending AL champion four years earlier? Have to be pretty weak in both math and history to fail to net this two-bagger.

5. He set an all-time rookie record when he lost 41 games for Indianapolis of the American Association in 1884. What's worse, he overtaxed his arm and was history soon thereafter. Two-run homer.

6. Representing the tying run, he ended the 1926 World Series and became a goat when he attempted to steal second base with Bob Meusel at bat and was cut down by Bob O'Farrell. Double.

7. He served up the three-run homer by Bucky Dent that catapulted the Yankees to the AL East flag in 1978. RBI single.

8. What Hall of Famer's career was wrecked when Earl Averill's line drive broke his toe in the 1937 All-Star Game and he tried to return to action before the injury had healed? Single.

9. He made three successive errors to undo Koufax in the game that marked Sandy's last major league appearance. RBI double.

10. The AL's winning-percentage leader in 1914 with a dazzling 17–3 record, he balked at the salary the A's offered him for 1915 and jumped to the Federal League, where he fell to 4–16, the worst mark in the FL. RBI triple.

11. He surrendered Maris's 61st homer in 1962. Too well-known to rate more than a single.

12. His first relief stint in the majors came in 1944 when he was 18; seven years later he made one of the most crucial relief appearances in history and saw every-

thing else he accomplished during his career, including a 21-win season in 1947, obliterated by one swing of the bat. Single for him; RBI for the man whose swing victimized him.

13. Cubs rooters and bench jockeys fell instantly still when he served up Ruth's "called shot" in the 3rd game of the 1932 World Series. Two-bagger.

14. This hurler gave up both the Babe's first and second career home runs in 1915. Ironically, he pitched for the Yankees, and knowing that should enable you to hop on this one for a homer of your own.

15. In their first four seasons of existence the Mets had at least one 20-game loser every year; all told, four different pitchers suffered that indignity during that span. Name all four for a homer; double for three; sac hit for less—unless of course you don't know any of them!

SCORING CHART

Potential Total Bases: 30	At-Bats: 15
	Hits:
Potential RBIS: 12	RBIS:
	Total Bases:

26. Forget Me Not

This one doesn't require much explanation. What we have here are 15 good ball players, some of them perhaps even great, who have been . . . But let's listen to them tell it in their own way.

1. My misfortune was to play the position that got no respect in the game's early days. Fact is, only one

man who played it prior to 1908 is in the Hall of
Fame. Too, I had the bad luck to manage the worst
major league team ever assembled—disassembled may
be more accurate—in my one crack at a helm post.
But I also played for some of the best teams of my
time, once held the record for the most career hits of
anyone who played my position, and no doubt will
always hold the distinction of being the only man to
play for four teams that represented the same city in
four different leagues. Two-bagger.

2. One of the best kept secrets is that the Veterans
Committee a couple of years back actually voted me
into the Hall of Fame and then reneged on it. When
I was in my prime, though, it was no secret that I
was a great pitcher trapped on a rotten team. Lost a
20th-century-record 54 games for those Beaneaters
over a two-year period before they took pity on me
and swapped me to Pittsburgh. Where I won 20 four
years running, only to have Clarke reward me by
shipping me off to the Cardinals, another tail-ender
at the time. Can't blame me for quitting after one
fruitless year with them or for believing I'd have won
300 easy if my rubber arm had toiled for the right
team all along. RBI single.

3. They said my glove was a joke and my eccentricities
would do me in. Well, they did eventually, but it
wasn't that I was such an oddball so much as that I
was nigh deaf. That didn't come out until later, of
course, when I was gone, and by then nobody still
cared that I and Brouthers were tied with the highest
career batting averages among hitters who did most
of their swinging at pitches that were thrown from
only 50 feet away. Nobody wants to believe either
that I played in a circuit every bit as strong as the NL
or that the batting crown I snagged in the Players
League—against the top pitchers from both my circuit and the NL—proved my mettle as a batsman
once and for all. Well, my nephew Tod can still ring
a few chimes whenever that great film of his, *Freaks*,

is shown even if everybody's turned ears deafer than my own to all I did to glorify the family name back then. Single.

4. Hey, we've each won at least four batting crowns (one of us has five) but never have been selected MVPs. What's a man have to do to get a little recognition when he's playing the position that now has about ten future Hall of Famers to every one it had a century earlier? Need both for a single.

5. The Phils thought I was all done in '21 when all I could do for them was hit .321—I guess because I didn't feature the kind of power that other first sackers were showing now that the ball had been juiced. Little did they or anybody else know that I still had a lot of big years left in the minors, and I do mean big. Like that .341 for Fort Worth in '25 with 41 homers and 166 ribbies, both tops in the Texas circuit. 'Course I was 40 by then, but still I'd have liked to return to the majors, get another eight RBIs to make an even 1,000, and maybe a few more triples to put me up around 200. But the stats I was always proudest of really were those fielding marks. Had the top FA for first sackers for a while and a flock of other glove records too. Wasn't much I couldn't do, when you come down to it, except change the fact that I came along about ten years too soon. Kelly and Bottomley and some of those other lively-ball era gateway guardians were good but no better than me. RBI double.

6. There's one Hall of Famer who made it because he was half of a famous brother act. So what's the case against me? I averaged nearly 105 runs in the ten full seasons I played—lost three to WWII that would have been among my best, too—and was the first AL outfielder to make 500 putouts in a season. Even my brother never did that. He hit the long ball, though, as did my other brother. But, cripes, was it my fault that the thing I could do just about the best of anyone in my era—steal bases—rated so low then?

That youth movement killed me too. Had another three or four years left when the Sox gave my job to Tommy Umphlett. Remember him? Guess I just made my point, didn't I? Single.

7. Well, I was part of a famous brother act too. But I also happened to play that ignored position back then. That is, when I wasn't back of the plate, where I started out as just about the first catcher to play right up behind a batter. Then I played on some mighty fine teams and usually hit above .300. What didn't I do that could account now for my still being outside the Hall of Fame? Can't think of a thing, unless it was that I believed the world was flat. Wouldn't imagine they'd hold that against a man all these long years, though, would you? Especially one who played until he was past 40 and had over 2,000 hits counting all those ones he made in the National Association. RBI single.

8. They didn't have a Cy Young Award when I pitched or I'd probably have won at least two. What I did win was 200 games and the distinction of posting the highest career batting average ever by a pitcher with over 1,000 at bats. Never'll get into the Hall of Fame, but at least I got into a Series and had the pleasure most of my career of playing right in my hometown. Had a son who looked for a time as if he'd make it, too, before he ran into some arm trouble in the minors. His laying on you what a great hitter he was makes this only a single.

9. That team I played for just never would hit enough to support me. Consequently I had the lowest career ERA of any pitcher who retired with a losing record. It was 2.30, my friend, and yet even in my best season I still lost more than I won. I was born in Deadwood, S.D., and they called me Death Valley Jim. I sure think they were right because there's something downright morbid when a man has a 1.90

ERA, even in the deadball year of 1913, and still
gets charged with 20 defeats. Oh, those hitless wonders! RBI double.

10. Some'd say I was Death Valley Jim's counterpart
in the NL. A 2.89 career ERA that was blown
up some because I pitched my last few years with
a rabbit ball, but back at my peak I was the top
lefty in the senior circuit for years, though I couldn't
show it since I was with just about the NL's worst
team at the time. Those Pirates, wouldn't you
know that after 13 years with them I'd get sent
to the Cubs before the '25 season just when they
finally got it together to win? And where'd the
Cubs finish in '25? Yep, you got it. Dead last.
Three-bagger.

11. Made a fatal mistake in 1903 when I jumped the
White Sox to join McGraw's Giants. Was forced to
sit out nearly the whole season before going back to
the Sox and lost the 140 or so hits I'd otherwise have
had, which would have put me up well over 2,800
career-wise. Even at that, though, I had the most
hits of any switch sticker in history prior to Mickey
Mantle and was the first shortstop ever to be a
league leader in RBIs. Got a lot of triples and stolen
bases too. Wagner was my only clear superior then,
and there have been a lot of my inferiors since who
now are where I, too, belong—in Cooperstown. RBI
single.

12. You know, maybe that guy wasn't wrong when he
voted me the MVP in '67 to deprive Yaz of being
a unanimous choice. I really did do a bundle for
the Twins that year, even if I didn't hit my peak
until later on. Anyway, I gave the game all I had
and could play just about anywhere they put me
too. Never made 2,000 hits or got into a Series,
but that's no excuse for forgetting I was one solid
ball player, man, day in and out for nearly a decade.
Double.

13. Won't have to do more to make my case that I was
the best player on the original Red Stockings than
bid you to look at my career stats. Too bad in retrospect that I quit while at the top of my game and
went out to the West Coast to do engineering. About
the only place I couldn't fill on the diamond field was
shortstop, but of course I was never tried there either. Still, I had 11 solid years of ball and hit around
.345 all told, I'd reckon. Triple.

14. Probably you've seen a picture of me with a handle-
bar mustache, since I was the last player in the
majors to sport one until the '70s. But go take a look
at those 11 years I played during the deadball era for
the Phils and Braves. Steady was my middle name.
Only one bad year, that in '09, and twice got over
the .300 figure. I'd say I was among the top six or
seven outfielders in the NL during my time, wouldn't
you? Home run.

15. There were an awful lot of great center fielders when
I played. Three or four of them are in the Hall of
Fame, and a couple more probably should be. Not
saying I'm one of them because I'll be the first to
admit it—I struck out too often to fashion the sort of
batting averages you needed in the '50s to interest
voters now. But I'll match every other phase of my
game against anybody's—then or now. Always thought
I should have gotten the AL MVP award in '54 too.
If I'd hit about ten points higher, it would have been
a real crime to deny me. Well, I'll always have one
great and everlasting distinction at any rate. Got to
thank Bill Veeck for that and then Boudreau and
Gordon for seeing pretty quickly that I wasn't really
cut out for second base. RBI single.

SCORING CHART

Potential Total Bases: 26	At-Bats: 15
	Hits:
Potential RBIS: 7	RBIS:
	Total Bases:

27. Their Niche Is Secure

1. He holds the record for the most innings pitched in a season between the end of the deadball era and the end of the 154-game schedule. Two-bagger.

2. He retired in 1985 with only one career home run—the fewest by an NL player with over 3,000 career at bats. Mere single for this singular flea-swatter.

3. This fading flower hit a robust .175 in 1886 for the Kansas City Cowboys of the National League. It ranks as the lowest average ever by an outfielder with over 400 at-bats, and his .197 slugging average that year set an additional mark. Unless you've heard me give this one on the radio, you're a poor bet to nail a grand slam homer.

4. His .538 slugging average in 1931 stands as the highest by an NL player in his final big league season; moreover, it was his only campaign in top company despite minor league stats that should have assured all but the comatose that his rookie showing was no mirage. RBI double.

5. This Cleveland bullpenner, who was felled by heart trouble after the 1948 season, had his all-time record for the most saves (17) by a pitcher in his final year tied by Rollie Fingers in 1985. Solo homer.

6. He finished with 3,630 hits, the most by a player who spent his entire career with one team. Single.

7. He is the only starting pitcher to put in 20 years in the majors without ever collecting 100 strikeouts in a season. His best was 74 in 1933. Announcing he's in the Hall of Fame should spur you to go for this RBI double.

8. He had a 1–10 record for the 1902 Baltimore Orioles, then set an OB record when he dropped 62 games during the next two seasons while with Portland in the Pacific Coast League. Rates a three-run homer.

9. In 1915 he became the first lefty to win 300 games. Just a single for him, but make it a homer if you know the team whose uniform he wore when he did it.

10. He umpired in the majors a record 37 seasons and 18 World Series. Single.

11. This Cinci control artist was the NL's top pitcher in 1922–26 with 96 wins. He tailed off sharply after that, however, which is why he'll never join others who were less successful during that five-year span in the Hall of Fame, and you'll hook a triple if you get him.

12. He worked an all-time record 188 consecutive complete games over a five-year period before Brooklyn knocked him out of the box near the end of the 1906 season. Double.

13. At the opposite end of the continuum, this Braves righty set an all-time futility record when he made 37 starts in 1985 without a single complete game. Hearing that he's since set an all-time positive pitching mark for another team should aid you to an RBI single.

14. He won only 89 games in the majors, but set an AL record when he launched his career by winning 20 games in each of his first three seasons. With Cleveland at the time, he finished with the 1925 Senators. Worth a run-scoring double.

15. He is the only 300-game winner who never pitched on a pennant winner or from a pitcher's box more than 50 feet from home plate. Historians will bank an easy double; the rest of you may get lucky and guess right.

SCORING CHART

Potential Total Bases: 35	At-Bats: 15
	Hits:
Potential RBIS: 13	RBIS:
	Total Bases:

28. Minor League Maestros

1. Although he hit well in the majors—.305 in 473 games—his notoriously unreliable glove work caused first the White Sox and then the Red Sox to despair. In the minors, however, he hammered .366 over 16 seasons, won five batting titles, and quit in 1941 as the last player in OB whose overall career average rated out to be above .355. Get off to a mirthful beginning with an RBI single.

2. The Joe Sewell of the minor leagues, this outfielder fanned just three times in 1925 and less than 140 times in 1,943 games while hitting .324, mostly in the IL. He rapped .350 in the Piedmont League in 1920 when he was only 17 and quit when he was just 31, despondent that he never got a chance to showcase his magic bat in the majors. Three-run homer.

3. Probably the youngest player ever to top an OB league in a major offensive department, he led the Western Association in hits in 1934 when he was just 16. A year later this shortstop-third baseman was starring for Los Angeles in the PCL. Three seasons as the Reds third sacker during WWII constituted his only appreciable time in the majors, however, and the explanation usually given for his failure to stick up top was a lack of power. That it had considerable validity there can be no doubt; in 1952 he set one of the oddest records in post-deadball OB history when he led the Pioneer League in batting while hitting nary a triple or home run. Solo four-bagger.

4. After posting a glittering 26–6 mark for Fall River of the New England League in 1896, he nearly equaled it the following year when he was 26–7 with Boston and led the NL in winning percentage. He won just 21 more games in the majors, however, before slipping back to the lower echelons. Three-run homer.

5. He led the IL a record four times in home runs and was named the loop's MVP in 1947 when he gunned 53 out of the park for Baltimore, but an inability to handle benders doomed this outfielder-third sacker to an .097 career mark in the majors. Two-run homer.

6. Seven years after being named MVP by AL officials, in 1933 this 40-year-old Seattle first sacker still had enough stick to clobber PCL pitchers for 27 homers and 138 RBIs. One of the few minor league bammers you'll meet here who also starred in the majors—and an AL MVP no less—he's worth just a single, especially when I toss in that he once held the major league single-season record for doubles.

7. A terrible hitter in the majors, he averaged just .231 in 536 games, including a meager .206 as the A's right fielder in 1915. His problem, though, may simply have been that he was a late bloomer. Perhaps the only player in history who had nearly all his top

seasons when he was past 35, he led the IL in batting in 1925 when he was 40 and then repeated his feat the following year when he cracked .388. Retired after the 1931 season with a .316 career average in the minors, nearly 100 points above his major league figure. Three-run double.

8. This big righthander didn't start his pro career in earnest until 1904 when he was 32. After winning 99 games over the next three seasons in the low minors, he was acquired by the anemic-hitting Cardinals and made their workhorse in 1907. Disgusted when he led the NL with 25 losses despite posting a 2.91 ERA, he spent most of 1908 in the Cards' doghouse before joining Milwaukee in the AA. Three more outstanding seasons with the Brewers made it clear that he might have been something extraordinary if he'd turned pro sooner. As it was, he was merely spectacular, and so will you be if you homer here.

9. In 1922 this former Tigers reliever became the last pitcher in OB history to win more than 35 games in a season when he logged a 38–13 record for Tulsa of the Western League and fanned 333 batters in 441 innings. The owner of a truly bizarre career—he pitched nine years in the majors, but never more than 63 innings in a season—he'll bring an RBI triple.

10. Between 1938 and 1941 he copped an OB-record four batting titles in four different leagues. Come 1942 he hit .300 for the Cubs in his first full year in the majors. Alas, it turned out to be his only solid season up top, although he later had several more fine ones in the PCL. Make you mad if you miss this two-bagger.

11. This outfielder failed to connect with the White Sox in the mid-'20s but went on to bag a record 3,617 hits, 2,286 runs, and 743 doubles in the minors, most of them in the AA and the PCL, before calling it a

career after the 1948 season. Strangely enough, just about the only thing he missed collecting in his long career was a batting title. RBI single.

12. His two legs helped carry him to the MVP award in the Southern Association in 1944 when he rapped .333 and swiped 68 bases. The next year the fact that he had only one arm carried him to a full season in the majors as a wartime drawing card. Should prove to be a cinch single.

13. This ex-Giants relief whiz won only one more game in the majors after he rattled off 21 victories in 1915 for the St. Louis Terriers of the Federal League. But he spent the next 14 years winning 235 games in the minors, most of them in the PCL. An outstanding hitter and infielder to boot, he was originally snatched by the Terriers to play second base before his arm made it apparent McGraw may have errored using him mainly in the bullpen. Need a doctor if you miss a homer here.

14. He hit .412 for Baltimore in 1921, made an IL-record 246 hits, and had a 12–1 mark on the mound. Two years later, after being purchased by the Giants, he broke in by winning 13 games and stroking .427 as a pitcher-pinch hitter. RBI double for this minor league great and jack-of-all-trades.

15. His .366 career average is the highest of anyone in OB history, even above Ty Cobb's whose was *lowered* by his minor league stats. Unfortunately this lefty opposite-field hitter achieved almost all of it in the PCL, where he swept a record four batting titles in the 1930s, three of them in a row. In 1935, playing with the Mission Reds, he hit .399 to top a young Joe DiMaggio of the other San Francisco PCL entry, the Seals. Double for a man whose nickname gave the erroneous impression he was a power hitter.

SCORING CHART

Potential
Total Bases: 39

Potential
RBIS: 18

At-Bats: 15

Hits:

RBIS:

Total Bases:

August

The Magic Year

Of the seven players in major league history who have had seasons in which they amassed 420 or more total bases, six did it between 1921 and 1932, a period when the balance scale was tipped decidedly in the favor of hitters and almost every important single-season batting record was established. Only one man subsequent to 1932 fashioned a season loaded with the kind of offensive stats that have otherwise been seen only in the 12-year period immediately after the lively ball was first introduced.

In some respects, our man's season is the most extraordinary that any hitter has ever enjoyed. Yet it is seldom cited as one of the all-time great batting feats. The reasons for that are twofold. First, he broke no records that year—he didn't even come close to breaking any. Furthermore, he failed to win the Triple Crown, missing out by a margin of one home run.

Had he hit just one more homer, he would not only have bagged the Triple Crown, he would have led his league in every major offensive department except walks and stolen bases. As it is, he topped his circuit in eight departments! More than that, as the following chart shows, he produced figures that in each case towered over those of his closest rival.

Department	Our Man	Runner-up
Batting Average	.376	.333
Slugging Average	.702	.564
RBIs	131	125
Hits	230	190
Runs	135	117
Doubles	46	40
Triples	18	12
Total Bases	429	316

Many players have had seasons when they've led two or three batting departments by as wide a margin as our man's. Some have even led a couple of departments by wider margins. But no other player has ever so comfortably led eight departments, let alone come within a single home run of leading a ninth. For an RBI single, who is the man under consideration here, and what year did he work his magic? You need both to score.

29. Black Is Beautiful

1. Two years after Elston Howard broke the Yankees color barrier, he became the second black player to wear pinstripes. Pack away a three-bagger.

2. He is the lone black switch hitter to win an AL MVP Award. Warn you this one'll be rugged unless you happen to know it off the top of your head. RBI double.

3. They were the first team to feature an all-black keystone combo. Single for the team; two bases if you know the year and both players too.

4. What black catcher who never played in the majors is considered by many to have been as good as, if not better than Campanella? Single.

5. He was the first black to win back-to-back batting titles. Single.

6. He claimed to be Cuban, but may actually have been the first black to play in the majors. In any case, he was the first San Franciscan, debuting in 1882 with Providence. Flummoxed by overhand pitching and the departure of his favorite battery mate, Charlie Sweeney, a fellow San Franciscan, he hit a paltry .095 in 1884 and was gone soon thereafter. Two-run homer for you if you're aware of this little-known sidebar in the history of the 1880s.

7. Now known to have been at least 35 when he arrived in the majors, he shaved several years off his birth date in order to get the chance to crack 28 homers and 107 RBIs in 1950, his first year as a regular first sacker. Double.

8. He was the first black to win an AL MVP Award. Single for him; ribby for the year he did it.

9. The first black World Series was held in 1924 and won by the Kansas City Monarchs, the Negro Western League champs, over Hillsdale of Philadelphia, the Eastern Colored League champs, 5–4 in the best of nine games. What star shortstop for the Bacharach Giants, who was called the "black Wagner," won the ECL bat crown that year with a .444 average? Two-run triple.

10. Analysts point to one season as the turning point in the ever increasing disparity between the NL and the AL with the respect to talented black players. In that campaign blacks led every major batting department in the NL but one (bases on balls) while only Floyd Robinson (doubles) was an AL leader. For a two-bagger, what year are we talking about?

11. The premier black pitcher prior to 1900, he won 35 games for Newark of the Eastern League (the forerunner of the modern-day International League) in 1887 to set an all-time loop record. RBI double.

12. Name the black pitcher, known as the "Cuban Matty," whom John McGraw and the Giants were prevented by the other major league clubs from signing in the early 1900s. Two-run homer.

13. In 1974 every team in the NL West had a black or Latin center fielder except for the cellar dwellers. Who were they and who played center field for them? Need both for an RBI double.

14. He was the first black to win a minor league batting crown in this century. His name, the year he did it, and the team he played for are worth a two-run double. A mere sac hit for anything less than that.

15. Sure, you probably know that the Red Sox were the last major league team to integrate, but I'll stake a homer that you don't know the first black to play major league ball in a Boston uniform.

SCORING CHART

Potential Total Bases: 35	At-Bats: 15
	Hits:
Potential RBIS: 13	RBIS:
	Total Bases:

30. Fabled Freshmen

1. Grab a bingle for naming the speedster whose NL rookie stolen-base mark Vince Coleman broke in 1985. And an RBI for the year he did it.

2. After a long career in the PCL, this 31-year-old righty was given a belated shot in 1924 by the Pirates and won 18 games while leading the NL in shutouts; before departing nine years later, he collected 143 victories, all with Pittsburgh, and twice led the NL in wins. Two-run double.

3. He debuted as a pro with a 20–11 record for Lancaster of the Interstate League in 1943. Given a chance by the apathetic Athletics two years later, he fashioned an 0–12 mark in his lone taste of big league life. In 1947, however, he rebounded to post a 10–2 record as a reliever for Minneapolis and set a new

AA record when he appeared in 83 games. That 0–12 debut alone will allow 40s freaks to lap up an easy triple.

4. In 1943 this Tigers shortstop became the first AL rookie to fan over 100 times; in addition, he set an AL rookie mark for the most sacrifices with no sacrifice flies. Vacuum up a two-run homer for a man last seen in the 1945 World Series.

5. Only a single for the first AL Rookie of the Year to subsequently win a batting crown. With an RBI for the year he copped frosh honors.

6. And another single for the first AL Rookie of the Year to subsequently win an MVP award. But to get an RBI you need *both* years he took honors.

7. In 1921, while batting just .248 and collecting only nine stolen bases, this Phillies frosh set a post-1900 NL rookie record (since broken) for the most consecutive games hitting safely (23) and the most times caught stealing (18). A homer for this paradoxical gold-striker.

8. He set all-time rookie standards when he swiped 98 bases and scored 152 runs for Baltimore of the American Association in 1887. If told that he led all NL outfielders in fielding five times in the 1890s, you should score a two-run deuce.

9. The only yearling 20-game winner to cop rookie honors in the AL, he's also the lone pitcher in big league history to win 20 games pitching fewer than 200 innings. Record mavens would frown if I gave more than a double here.

10. For years he was considered to have been the first rookie to win a major league bat title, but most record books now credit him with the second-best average to Paul Hines's .358. A double for his name, plus an RBI for his frosh year.

11. Well then, who was the first rook to win a bat title?
None other than the first player to have his bats custom-
made. That clue alone should bring a quick single.

12. If Rookie of the Year honors had been awarded
back in 1919, he would have won in the NL by
default (there were no other contenders) with a .226
batting average in 190 at-bats. Shouldn't be a hard
double once you're told he's in the Hall of Fame.

13. What team had three pitchers in a row cop Rookie of
the Year honors? The team's worth a single; the
exact years it happened an RBI; and you've bagged
another RBI if you know all three hurlers.

14. The opposite of the above club, which has had many
rookie winners, this team is the lone franchise that's
been in existence ever since the frosh award was
started in 1947 that has yet to have the top rookie in
its league. Single.

15. In 1890 this Cincinnati hurler launched his rookie
season with a 13–1 start and hung on to post the
NL's top ERA. The clue that he's the lone pitcher to
be an ERA leader both before and after the mound
was moved to its present distance from home plate
makes this one go for just a two-run triple.

16. Crack a three-run double for knowing the only player
since the inception of the Rookie of the Year Award
who hit .320+, scored 100+ runs, and had 200+
hits as a frosh, yet failed to cop the yearling honor.

SCORING CHART

Potential Total Bases: 32	At-Bats: 16
	Hits:
Potential RBIS: 18	RBIS:
	Total Bases:

31. Moments to Remember

1. He's the only man in history to homer in his first big league at-bat while wearing a Yankees uniform. His only other homer came in—what else?—a Dodgers suit. A homer in its own right, and with two on, no less.

2. When told the first player in big league history to bag 100 or more RBIs in each of his first two seasons was a shortstop, you should go right on to collect a stand-up double.

3. Still active in 1990, he's the last player to have a season in which he led the majors in hits, runs, and triples; for an RBI single your only clue is that he tied for the top in three-baggers.

4. He gave Walter Johnson and the Senators some much needed mound help— and instant respectability—when he won 17 games as a rookie in 1913, including his first 11 decisions. Two-run triple.

5. When he retired in 1953 with a .312 career average, who could have known he'd be the last player to quit with a .300+ average after ten or more seasons while wearing Cleveland garb? Even those aware that the Indians were once rife with great hitters may stumble trying for two here.

6. Credit another double if you know the Hall of Famer who was the last player to retire with a 300+ career average after ten or more seasons while wearing Yankees livery.

7. He is the lone player to retire in a Mets uniform with a .300+ career average in ten or more seasons, one of which included a .300 season with the Mets. Worth an RBI double.

8. But a single's all you get for knowing the lone player who retired with a .330+ career average since the expansion era commenced.

9. Single again by nailing the last player to win back-to-back MVP awards. And chalk up an RBI if you know the years he did it.

10. Stretch this blooper into a double and name the former Cy Young winner who tossed away a strong chance to snag 200 career victories when he quit the game rather than go to an expansion team in 1969.

11. The Cards at one time had the game's best farm system and a long tradition of building powerful teams with its graduates. When they returned to the top in 1964 after an 18-year drought, who were their only two regulars (300 or more at-bats) who came up through their chain? A double for knowing both, but just a sac hit and no time at bat if you get only one.

12. His record for being the lone righthanded batter to hit .410 or better in the AL could not possibly have stood any longer than it has. That clue makes this almost a giveaway single.

13. You could have gotten long odds that this slugger would one day be a shoo-in to make the Hall of Fame after he hit a meager .196 and fanned 136 times in just 367 at-bats as a rookie. RBI single.

14. He had the greatest season of any pitcher in OB history involved in 25 or more decisions when he posted a 25–1 record for Salisbury in the Eastern Shore League and then won a complete-game start with Washington to finish the 1937 season at 26–1. Being told he never won another game in the majors should explain why this ranks as a grand slam.

15. By age 24 he had 180 wins. He won only 13 more, but one of his triumphs, in 1884, ended the St. Louis

Maroons' all-time record of 20 consecutive victories to open the season. Could score a gilt-edged two-run homer here.

SCORING CHART

Potential	At-Bats: 15
Total Bases: 32	
	Hits:
Potential	
RBIS: 14	RBIS:
	Total Bases:

32. Team Teasers

1. They were the first team to slam more than 200 home runs and win more than 100 games in the same season. Learning you'll snag a two-run double for the team and year should caution you this one's no cinch.

2. They were the last NL team to win back-to-back World Championships. You're on your honor not to grant yourself a single if it takes you longer than ten seconds to score here.

3. The first team to win a flag without a 20-game winner, .300 hitter, or 100-RBI man, they narrowly missed taking the World Championship before losing to an AL club that also lacked a .300 hitter. Two-bagger.

4. The last team to win back-to-back World Championships had just one regular (300 or more at-bats) who hit .300 both seasons. Given the clue that in the latter campaign he played over 100 games in the field for the first time in four years, you ought to nail both the club and the player for an RBI single. Zip, though, if you don't get him.

5. What was the only team that failed to win an pennant despite having four 20-game winners? Two bases for the team and year; three RBIs for all four hurlers; two RBIs for three hurlers; no ribbies for less.

6. This team remained in the hunt during the late 1930s without a single pitcher who worked as many as 200 innings. When rookie Dick Newsome topped 200 in 1941, he became the club's first hurler to do it since 1937. Name 'em for three.

7. The last Padres hurler and the last Indians hurler to win 20 games in a season is one and the same pitcher. Single.

8. What team posted a .212 batting average and .261 slugging average, both of which are 20th-century record lows? If told its slugging leader was Patsy Dougherty with a .300 SA—85 points below Ty Cobb's *batting* average that season— can you homer by naming both the club and the year? Single for just the club.

9. In their inaugural season they were called the Broncos, the next year they became the Blues, and for a while, before adopting their present nickname, they were also known as the Molly McGuires. RBI double.

10. Fans in this city gloated when its teams won five World Championships in seven years, but it's now been seven full decades since a pitcher on a club representing that once-supreme baseball town has won the last game of a World Series. For a two-run double, name him; sac hit for knowing just the city we're talking about.

11. Only once since the advent of the 154-game schedule have two teams in the same league lost fewer than 50 games. In which circuit did it happen, who won the pennant that year, and which club finished second

with the highest winning percentage in modern history by an also-ran? Need all for a homer; sac hit for less.

12. What team in this century hit .315, scored 944 runs, and finished in last place with a .338 winning percentage? Team and year are both necessary to get an RBI single here.

13. They won back-to-back pennants and had four 20-game losers in back-to-back seasons within a nine-year period. The club that went from the sublime to the ridiculous so quickly rates a double, plus two ribbies if you know the exact years the outfit accomplished this paradoxical feat.

14. Worth another double if you know the first team to win three consecutive flags in the 20th century and an RBI for the exact years it was done.

15. What team set a record when it finished in the first division (fourth place) with a .448 winning percentage, and then set another record the following year when it won 15 more games and yet failed to advance a single notch in the standings? Triple for the club; three RBIs for the years it tread water with 69–85 and 84–68 marks respectively.

SCORING CHART

Potential Total Bases: 32	At-Bats: 15
	Hits:
Potential RBIS: 17	RBIS:
	Total Bases:

33. The Evolving Game

One of the great things about baseball, as contrasted to other sports, is how changeless it is. The game's the same basically as it was in its infancy. Yet there have been some significant alterations down through the years. Let's just test how aware you are of them.

1. Like the pitcher's mound. What was the first season it was stationed at its present distance from home plate? That's worth only a sac hit, though, unless you can explain in 50 words or less why it's now 60'6" from the plate rather than an even 60 feet. Credit a homer if you're right.

2. A 154-game schedule was adopted briefly in 1892 when the NL first swelled to 12 teams. What year did the 154-game schedule become the standard in both major leagues that lasted until expansion? Two bases.

3. Now all you have to know is when expansion bade both leagues to adopt the present 162-game schedule. Careful now, what we're looking for is the year *both* leagues began playing eight more games a season. Single.

4. When the American Association claimed major league status in 1882, what three perks did it offer fans that the stodgy National League refused to provide? Triple for all three; double for two; sac hit for just one.

5. Of course, the term "fan" wasn't yet in currency in 1882—the game's followers were known as cranks. What club owner and his manager are generally credited with coining the term? Hint: it was a shortened form of fanatic. RBI triple.

6. What was the first season that foul balls were counted as strikes by both major leagues? Double, plus an RBI for the season fouls began counting as strikes in just one league.

7. What was the last of the original 16 major league teams to play a home game on Sunday? Two bases, plus two ribbies for the year it happened.

8. Prior to 1900, what was the shape of home plate? RBI single.

9. What zany player is generally considered to have been responsible for a rule being written that the bases could not be run in reverse order? Triple.

10. This bespectacled righty, the first player in history to wear glasses, and an obscure pitcher named Jack Schappert had pivotal roles in forcing a rule to be written that hurlers could no longer hit batters at will without penalty. Clues make this so simple I hate to give even a single.

11. What was the first season that pitchers in all leagues, major and minor, were allowed to throw overhand? Rates a triple if only because you need more than a cursory knowledge of rule changes to know this alteration was done in stages.

12. What rule change in 1891 made possible the use of pinch hitters? RBI single.

13. What do Paul Waner's .336 batting average in 1926, Eddie Collins's .344 BA in 1914, Stan Hack's .317 BA in 1940, and Ted Williams's .345 BA in 1954 have in common? Seemingly nothing except that they all were achieved in even years, but I'll be amazed if you don't hone in pretty quickly on their shared denominator. Double.

14. The 1921 World Series is famous for being the first "Subway Series." Not so well remembered is that it was also the last time that something was done in a Series. For a double, what was it? Hint: it was also done in the 1903, 1919, and 1920 World Series, but not in any of the Series played between 1905 and 1918.

15. What was the first season that both leagues divided
    into two divisions and began playing a League Cham-
    pionship Series at the conclusion of the regular sea-
    son? Single.

SCORING CHART

Potential Total Bases: 32	At-Bats: 15
	Hits:
Potential RBIS: 17	RBIS:
	Total Bases:

34. Men of Mystery

All of these men had careers that raised puzzling questions that in most cases still await satisfactory explanation.

1. The encyclopedia's full of players who had one super
   season and could never repeat it. He had two back-
   to-back, however, hitting .344 and .340 before inex-
   plicably fading to mediocrity. Called "Beau" because
   of his penchant for girls of Bohemian extraction, he
   led the AL in hits and doubles in 1937 with the
   cellar-dwelling Browns; three years later he held down
   right field for the Cry Babies in his last fling as a
   regular. RBI double.

2. He had an eye-popping 77–25 career record after his
   first three seasons, then was sent to Pittsburgh when
   he got off to a rocky start in 1898. He won only 14
   more games, but had the distinction of being Cleveland's starting pitcher in the AL's inaugural game.
   The last pitcher to win 30 games as a rookie, he was
   so embittered by the treatment the Orioles accorded
   him after he'd been their ace for three years that he
   never again set foot in Baltimore, although he lived
   to be nearly 89. Two-run double.

3. Many great minor league hitters have fizzled when they were tested up top, but this lefty-swinging first baseman-outfielder notched a .301 career average in 320 games. The holder of the American Association record for the most hits in a season, set in 1921, he had the unique experience, six years earlier, of playing for a minor league team and a major league team in the same city in the same season—and hitting better for the major league crew (.310 to .286). Yet unaccountably, except for a handful of games with the 1918 Yankees, that was his last fling in the majors. Triple.

4. In 1947 he racked up 137 walks and was high among the AL home run leaders, but got a pink slip from the Tigers when his batting average dipped 111 points from his 1946 mark of .335, a personal best. In result he left with the record for the most bases on balls by a player in his final season—as well as the most, to that point, by a switch hitter. Knowing about those two records, you should double.

5. Reputedly he had the best stuff of any NL lefty in the late '40s. He was determined to pitch his own way, however, and when you were on a team managed by somebody like Durocher, sooner or later that kind of attitude put you between a rock and a very hard place. For this Virginian the end came much sooner than it should have. He led the NL in walks as a rookie in 1946, won a personal high 12 games in 1949, and finished in 1953 as a middle reliever. Ott predicted stardom for him, but 40 years later he isn't even remembered as the great phenom from his team that never panned out. Clint Hartung was that, although at the time our man was rated every bit as highly as he was. Solo homer.

6. In 1898 he hit .322 in the Eastern League (later the IL) and found himself back in the EL in 1904 with Jersey City. During the intervening five seasons he was in the majors with five different teams and un-

able to settle down with any of them despite hitting
.300 or better every year and showing good power.
A fine base thief in addition—he led the EL in
1905—only his suspect glove, which accumulated 97
errors as Baltimore's shortstop in 1901, offers any
clue at this late date for why the AL's three-base-hit
leader in its inaugural season was cut after leading
the Phils in RBIs in his last major league campaign.
RBI triple.

7. In a career that spanned more than ten seasons and
   was laden with paradoxes, he saw regular duty at
   first base, third base, and the outfield and was also
   frequently used as a DH. His zenith came with the
   1979 Mariners when he ripped 20 homers while fanning just 35 times—an almost unbelievably low number for a slugger in the current era. As a rookie with
   the 1975 Tigers he whiffed even less—a mere 25
   times in 470 at-bats. His problem was that despite
   being a superb contact hitter with good speed, he
   could never seem to hit with anywhere near the
   consistency he displayed in the minors. Your guess
   why is probably as good as those offered by his many
   batting coaches. Single.

8. The rap on him was that he was an atrocious fielder
   with little power, but the rest of his game was excel-
   lent. In 1948 this third sacker led the AL in hits and
   also in steals for what would be the second of three
   consecutive seasons. Dropped by the White Sox after
   he hit .301 for them in 1951, he played for several
   years in the PCL before departing with a .306 career
   average and the distinction of being the last St. Louis
   Browns player to lead the AL in a major offensive
   department. RBI double.

9. Not much is known about this Canadian-born outfielder, except that he hit everywhere he went and
   that the Red Sox mysteriously cut him after he led
   the club in batting in 1907. A year earlier, in his only
   other season as a big league regular, he hit .320 for

Cleveland and finished fourth in the AL batting race. A two-time Western League batting champ—in 1903 and 1904—he quit in 1914 on the eve of his 40th birthday after rapping .335 for Omaha in the WL. Two-run triple.

10. This slugger's career was one of constant peaks and valleys with the latter predominating, so much so that he ended with a .244 career average in 1,765 games. His nadir came in 1974 when he hit all of .171 as a DH and had but 43 RBIs, this after leading the NL with 130 ribbies nine years earlier while with the Reds. That he hung on for 16 years was something of a marvel, considering that he was a Dave Kingman prototype in an era when the Kingmans hadn't yet become a valued fixture on the scene. RBI single.

11. Given a trial as a pitcher-outfielder by the drab 1915 Athletics, he gave up a record 16 walks in his lone complete game and showed zilch at the plate also, hitting just .056. He never again got back to the majors despite starring for years in the minors— his last appearance came in 1946 when he was 55 years old—mostly in the AA with St. Paul, for whom he played 11 seasons. Grid fans should nail him for a solo homer when told he played in the NFL in 1921 after hitting .324 for the Saints that season.

12. After helping to pitch the White Sox to the AL flag in 1901, he held down the club's third-base slot two years later before finding what seemed a permanent home in the outfield. Prior to the 1906 season, however, he stunned the Chisox by quitting to become the player-manager of the Logan Squares, a Windy City semi-pro team. Away from the majors for five years, he returned in 1911 as the Sox regular left fielder and then became the team's player-manager the following seasons. The possessor of one of the truly strange careers, in 1897 he had

the distinction of being the last rookie to qualify for both a batting title and an ERA crown as he won 12 games and hit .292 in 360 at-bats. One-run double.

13. Thirteen seems the perfect number of mystery men, and he's the perfect one to end on. His .333 career average is the highest of any player active ten or more seasons during the deadball era (save for Joe Jackson) who is not presently in the Hall of Fame. The kicker is that he seldom put in a full season without either being suspended or jumping his club or, as happened in 1902, spending a few months in jail. Married to Mabel Hite, a famed singer during the early part of the century who died young of cancer, he took to the boards himself for a while, but never with anywhere near the success he had in baseball. The only player ever to be a batting crown runner-up in both major leagues, he peaked in 1905 when he ripped .356 for the Giants and then had only one more full season, that in 1908, before departing for keeps six years later. Even with all the time he missed, he is rated among the top five players of the deadball era by many observers. Your rating, though, will dwindle to near zero if you don't take an RBI single here.

SCORING CHART

Potential	At-Bats: 13
Total Bases: 30	
	Hits:
Potential	
RBIS: 12	RBIS:
	Total Bases:

35. Their Niche Is Secure

1. He is the only player in AL history to get at least 200 hits, 40 doubles, 20 triples, and 20 homers in the same season. Two bases for him and two RBIs for the year he did it. Gift clue: he won a bat crown the following year.

2. This 300-game winner holds the NL record for the most seasons leading all senior loop hurlers in losses. RBI single.

3. He left the majors in 1981 with a .161 career average, the lowest ever by a player other than a catcher or a pitcher with over 500 career at-bats. His nadir came in 1971 when he hit .166 as the Phillies half-time third baseman. Two-run triple.

4. Of his 152 hits in 1932, nearly 6 percent of them came in a single game. Math aces will need all of about two seconds to snare an RBI double here.

5. On June 15, 1965, this Tiger set a big league mark when he entered a game as a reliever and fanned the first seven batters he faced. After being told he left an indelible mark on the game, but not as a bullpenner, you should streak to a stand-up double.

6. In 1932 this 26-game winner went an entire season—and a record 327 innings—without uncorking a wild pitch or hitting a single batsman. RBI double.

7. Fatten up with a grand slam. In 1884, after jumping from the NL to the Union Association, he set an all-time record when he *averaged* 16 strikeouts over a consecutive three-game period. Don't be duped when I add that this hurler jumped back to the NL the following season and teamed with Hoss Radbourn.

8. The last AL lefty to win 25 games and the holder of the record for the highest winning percentage by a 25-game winner are one and the same hurler. Take a bingle for him and an RBI for the year his stats glittered so brightly.

9. Although he retired in 1920 with a .218 career batting average, the lowest ever by a player with over 3,000 at-bats, his glovework at shortstop helped the Big Train to many victories. Ample clues here to snatch an RBI double.

10. This home run leader's .225 career average is the lowest in history by an outfielder with over 3,000 at-bats. Hearing that he was seen last in the AL but not with the A's should steer you off the wrong low-average slugger. RBI single.

11. What southpaw pitcher set a 20th-century record for the fewest strikeouts by a leader in one major league circuit and subsequently set the record for the most strikeouts in a 154-game season in the other major league? Might have been tough if you hadn't gotten that second bit of info; now it should be a sure single.

12. In 1921 Babe Ruth collected a record 457 total bases. Who topped the NL 15 years earlier, in the heart of the deadball era, with 237 total bases, little more than half Ruth's amount and the lowest number ever by a league leader in a 154-game season? The clues that he had the NL's best batting average that season and just two home runs will help you to another single, plus two RBIs if you know who was the runner-up with 232 total bases.

13. He tied Goat Anderson's 64-year-old record for the fewest RBIs by a batting-title qualifier when he knocked home just 12 runs in 549 at-bats in 1971. RBI triple.

14. He held the NL career strikeout record before Carl-
    ton broke it. Might add that he led the senior circuit
    in K's just once. Single.

15. Now it's a common occurrence, but bet a two-run
    double you don't know the first man to homer in
    every major league park in use during his career.
    That he played but one full year in the NL and his
    peak four-bagger year was 1922, when he clouted 21,
    should be all you need to end with a bang.

SCORING CHART

Potential
Total Bases: 28

Potential
RBIS: 18

At-Bats: 15

Hits:

RBIS:

Total Bases:

September

Only Yesterday

By early 1957 rumblings that this city was on the verge of receiving a major league franchise became a ground swell. Realizing its final season may be at hand, the minor league team that represented the city proceeded to field one of the finest clubs in its long history. Helped by the Red Sox, its parent outfit, the team stockpiled a blend of former major league stars and highly regarded young prospects. Hired to manage the team was a former American League MVP second baseman, a winner wherever he went.

The second sacker piloted the team to its best year since 1946 and its final pennant. On September 15, 1957, a month after an official announcement was made that the city would receive a major league franchise the following season, its minor league contingent hosted the last Pacific Coast League game played in town, the nightcap of a Sunday doubleheader against the Sacramento Solons. With 15,484 fans looking on, the team's manager played second base, went two for three, and even pitched a little. With the pennant already clinched, the manager heightened the carnival atmosphere by starting his star 5'5" outfielder on the mound. To complete the 33-year-old tableau the score was 14–7, favor Sacramento, but few in attendance cared. The struggle begun in 1903 by Cal Ewing as a quest for recognition by organized baseball, and later joined by Charlie Graham and Paul Fagan, both of whom entertained far loftier ambitions, was finally over. When the 1958 season opened, this long-time Pacific Coast League bastion would at last be part of the major league scene.

For a single, what city are we talking about? Take an extra base for knowing its famous minor league stadium which became, albeit briefly, the home of its first major league franchise. And collect another base if you know the team's player-manager in 1957 after being told that two years later he skippered a major league team to its only serious pennant bid in the last 34 years. Finally, claim two RBIs if you can recall the name of the diminutive outfielder who started on the mound in the city's last Pacific Coast League game and went on, the following year, to become the American League Rookie of the Year.

36. Like Father Like Son

1. He's the only member of the 3,000-hit club with a son who later debuted with the same team he did. Can't get an RBI single here by saying Pete Rose and hoping I'll give credit for prescience.

2. He was the second player in major league history to play for a team managed by his father. Single.

3. They hold the distinction of being the only father-son pitching combo each to be a league leader in losses. Both had short stays up top, but the father went on for years and years in the minors. RBI triple, folks.

4. In 1951 he hit .231 as the Cubs shortstop; 26 years later his son hit .231 while shortstopping for the Twins. Need only one name here to score a bingle.

5. He hit .192 as a utility infielder for the 1961 Pirates; in 1984 his son hit .193 as a rookie shortstop for the Angels. Couldn't resist linking these two combos together, could I? Single.

6. No father-son combo has ever formed a battery in the majors, but he was caught by his son in 1953 while leading the Evangeline League in ERA at age 48; seven years earlier, with the White Sox, he'd led all AL relievers with 13 wins. RBI double.

7. They're one of the few father-son combos to play on a pennant winner for the same franchise; they did it, however, in cities over 3,000 miles apart. *Père* in addition led the NL in homers and RBIs the year his team broke through while *fils* was only a backup catcher who failed to appear in the World Series. Need both for a double.

8. He held down the White Sox first-base job for six seasons in the 1920s; his son strove unsuccessfully for years in the 1950s to claim the Pale Hose catching job. Worth a homer if you know both; father's only rated a single, though.

9. They're the only father-son combo each to be a league leader in pinch hits. Not the same league, but they've both got the same name. Three-bagger.

10. In 1938, en route to a short stint in the Phillies' outfield, he hit .310 for Seattle in the PCL; 30 years later, with hitting everywhere at its post-1920 nadir, his son led the Dodgers in home runs with ten. Solo homer.

11. He pitched on the same team with Walter Johnson and his brother once led the AL in pinch hits; he later sired two sons who were both NL batting leaders. Want the sons, too, of course, but without your knowing at least the father's nickname they're worth only a sac hit. With him, a double.

12. He caught Addie Joss in his initial big league season; some 26 years later his son caught the first large bonus paid to an unproven amateur and looked to be worth it when he led the AL in hits and doubles as a Tigers rookie in 1943. Name both for a triple; single for just the son.

13. He holds the major league record for the most consecutive games (18) with at least one RBI; his son suffered a career-curtailing injury that played a large

hand in there now being protective barriers in front of the first and third bases during batting practice. Oh, and by the by, the father had a twin brother who also played in the majors; both debuted, in fact, in 1920 after starring earlier in the year for Bridgeport of the Eastern League at first and second base respectively. Plenty there to jog you to an RBI double.

14. They were the first Latino father and son pair to make the majors. Both, as you might expect, played for the Senators. Solo homer.

15. He played regularly at three different positions; his son holds the major league record for the most games at still a fourth position. Can't be that anybody could need more than that to end with a quick single.

SCORING CHART

Potential Total Bases: 34	At-Bats: 15
	Hits:
Potential RBIS: 7	RBIS:
	Total Bases:

37. South of the Border

1. Known as "El Senor," he was the first Hispanic player to set a career record for the most games played at his position. Single.

2. He was the first Latino to win an MVP Award. RBI single; a second RBI if you nab the year he took the honor.

3. By winning 18 games for the 1943 Cubs and leading the NL in shutouts, he achieved the distinction of being the first Puerto Rican hurler to succeed in the

majors. The clue that the stadium in San Juan was later named for him posthumously should spur you to an RBI triple.

4. In 1951 these three Cuban-born right-handers formed the heart of the Senators' mound staff; all were gone from D.C. by 1954 when the best Cuban pitcher ever to wear Washington livery arrived on the scene. One base for each man; three-run homer if you know all four; but just a sac hit if you remember only the Senators ace in the late '50s.

5. In a few years there will probably be several, but at present he is the only Latino shortstop in the Hall of Fame. Single.

6. Nowadays it's a common occurrence, but take a double if you know the first year that two Latino shortstops faced each other in a World Series. Plus an RBI for nailing both of them and the teams they played for.

7. This Cuban switch hitter's theft of home in a late-season game in 1964 handed the Reds a 1–0 victory and started the Phillies on the slide that cost them what had seemed a certain pennant. Solo homer.

8. Take a single for naming the first Panamanian player to win a bat crown and an RBI for the year he first did it.

9. The first Cuban-born player to be a regular in either the NL or the AL in this century, he had two fine seasons with the Reds before jumping to the Federal League in 1914 and went into a tailspin thereafter. Primarily an outfielder, but he could play every infield position, too, if called on. Two-run homer.

10. He was the first Latino to be selected the NL Rookie of the Year. Single, plus and RBI for the year.

11. Who holds the record for the most career hits by a Cuban-born player? The steer that he holds a flock of other Cuban-born records as well should assure you of a single.

12. The A's top hitter during WWII, he jumped to the Mexican League in 1946 and was nearing 40 upon his reinstatement to OB in 1949. Only 5'6" tall, this Cuban packed a whallop—he hammered 32 homers for Minneapolis in 1940—and was in addition one of the smallest men ever to play first base in the majors. Played some third base also, but was mainly an outfielder. Two-run homer.

13. The only Latino regular on the 1973 NL champs, he sustained a broken collarbone four years later that helped end his career prematurely. RBI double.

14. The pride of Hwatabampo, Mexico, he set a major league record in 1937 when he scored nine runs for Washington in a doubleheader. Earlier he had starred in the PCL, as did his older brother, Louis, who never made the majors. Ample clues there to rope a two-run triple for this fleet outfielder.

15. A double's yours just for nailing the first Mexican-born player to win a major league batting title.

SCORING CHART

Potential	At-Bats: 15
Total Bases: 34	
	Hits:
Potential	
RBIS: 7	RBIS:
	Total Bases:

38. World War II Wrinkles

1. Several Hall of Famers played throughout the war. None, however, hit .300 all three wartime seasons. He came the closest, hitting .286 in 1943, winning a bat crown in 1944, and then rapping .306 in an injury-abbreviated 1945 season. Single.

2. He had his first winning season in ten years when he went 14–7 for the 1945 Giants in his big league coda and netted 101 strikeouts. Spent most of his career with the Giants' arch foe and you'll spend a sleepless night if this erstwhile whiff king doesn't add another double to your column.

3. Runner-up for the NL home run crown in 1945, he led the senior loop in pinch hits in 1946 before slipping to the minors, where he set an all-time Southern Association RBI record in 1948. He died of a bleeding ulcer in 1953, a few days prior to his 38th birthday. Run-scoring triple.

4. His 18 home runs in 1944 represented nearly 60 percent of the Senators' total of 33. A year later, with him in the service, Washington dropped to 27 homers and had just one in its home park, Griffith Stadium, that an inside-the-park job by first sacker _____. Two bases for filling in the blank; two bases for the 18-homer man in 1944—and a two-run homer if you snag both.

5. The only league leader in a major batting or pitching department in 1942 who never again played in the majors after his career was service-interrupted was the NL's winning percentage leader. If told he had a 15–4 record and threw a one-hitter in his final big league game, you should require no more to take an RBI double.

6. In 1945 the White Sox had both the second- and the third-best hitters in the AL. Neither ever played

another game in the majors. Name both and score three; single for knowing just one of them.

7. His 313 innings for the Giants in 1944 are the most by a rookie hurler since the end of the deadball era. The clues that he also led the NL in K's that year and won 21 games should bring you a double.

8. This 44-year-old bullpenner stood as an example of the many ancients who made good during the war after getting a belated opportunity when he had an 8–2 record in 1944 with 10 saves and a 1.96 ERA in 63 games for Cleveland. Homer.

9. The Cubs had no less than five catchers on their World Series roster in 1945. Which one did most of the work behind the plate for them during the fall classic? He hit .364, was last seen with the 1951 Dodgers, and rates a two-run homer.

10. After winning flags in 1942, 1943, and 1944, the Cards were heavily favored to win again in 1946 after all their vets returned. When they did, it became apparent that the absence of two stars from the 1944 team, who were lost to the service in 1945, in all likelihood cost them an NL record five straight pennants. Knowing both the missing stars can gain you an RBI double; sac hit if you nail only one.

11. In 1945, his swan song, this outfielder led the Red Sox in hits, RBIs, and homers while collecting his 2,000th career hit and—rather astonishingly—the lone pinch hit of his illustrious 13-year career. Telling you his brother hit .320 for the Red Sox in 1934 and collected 119 RBIs on just seven homers ought to make him a cinch two-bagger, and I'll throw in an RBI, too—provided, of course, that you get his brother as well.

12. And since we're on the subject of RBIs, this is a good place to finish. An RBI single's yours for nam-

ing the only man to collect 100 or more RBIs during each of the three war years. Only clue you should need is that he once won an MVP award—but not until after the war.

SCORING CHART

Potential Total Bases: 30	At-Bats: 12
	Hits:
Potential RBIS: 10	RBIS:
	Total Bases:

39. Now Batting For . . .

1. His 24 pinch hits in 1961 stood as the major league record until 1976 . . . and still stand as the record for a switch hitter. RBI single.

2. Inserted as a pinch hitter by the Senators with two out in the ninth and the Nats trailing Detroit 13–0, this ace at coming off the bench broke up Tommy Bridges' bid for a perfect game in 1932 with a single. The Bengals were furious that the Nats had called for the sheriff in a cause so hopeless. Two-run homer.

3. In 1943, three years after leading all AL pitchers in winning percentage, he led all NL hitters in pinch raps. Not a fluke by any means, either, Edna; he was one of the greatest all-around athletes ever to play the game. Triple.

4. This pitcher led the NL in pinch hits a record four times, three of them in succession (1929–31) and once held the career mark for the most pinch hits. Your face will be scarlet if you falter here. RBI single.

5. His .176 average is the lowest among players with over 200 career pinch-hit at-bats; he retired in 1970, seventeen years after he debuted in OB with a .432 mark for McAlester of the Sooner State League, a modern OB rookie record. Rates to be an RBI double.

6. In 1951, ten years after tying Debs Garms for the NL lead, he became the first ever to head both major leagues in pinch hits when he tied for the AL's top spot. If you don't know this and should happen to nail it with just a guess, you're either the luckiest or the shrewdest reader I've got, bud. Three-run triple.

7. In 1977 this Padres outfielder and present-day batting coach led the majors with 21 pinch hits and set a new single-season record for the most plate appearances by a pinch hitter (86). Two-run single.

8. His six pinch homers in 1932 toppled the old mark of three and still stand alone 58 years later. RBI single.

9. In 1892 he collected the first successful pinch hit in a major league game. The clues that he played for Cleveland then, made 1,822 career hits, and had a .301 career average make you still unlikely to score a bull's-eye guess. Either you already know enough to bag an RBI double or you don't.

10. He tied a World Series career record in 1954 when he cracked three pinch hits in his lone fall appearance. And in three at-bats. Double here or hit the road.

11. His 12 pinch hits for the White Sox in 1950 were the most in a season by any AL player between 1944 and 1953. Sounds a bit hard to believe, but you're welcome to look it up. Two-run homer.

12. He tied the NL record when he collected 22 pinch raps in 1962 and in addition became the first 2,000-hit club member to post as many as 20 in a season. RBI double.

13. For some inscrutable reason the Phillies used this outfielder frequently as a pinch hitter in the early 1950s. He gave them an .024 average coming off the bench, the lowest in history among players with 40 or more career pinch-hit at-bats. Can't deny that even '50s experts may find this three-run homer over their heads despite the clue that his last name and the *first* name of a Phils manager of the same vintage were the same.

14. Nothing esoteric, though, about this next guy. He debuted with the Pirates in 1954 and finished with them in 1966. During his 13-year career he averaged a solid nine pinch hits a season and retired with 116. Sharp single.

SCORING CHART

Potential Total Bases: 31	At-Bats: 14
	Hits:
Potential RBIS: 18	RBIS:
	Total Bases:

40. Their Niche Is Secure

1. No catcher has ever garnered 200 hits in a season. He came the closest with 193 in 1975. RBI single.

2. Still the co-holder of the record for the most triples in a season by a catcher, he at one time also held the mark for the most stolen bases by a backstopper. Quite a feat for a guy many of you are going to whiff on. Triple.

3. His 100 doubles for Tulsa of the Western League in 1924 are an all-time OB record. His only doubles in big league garb came with the 1920–21 Browns, which'll probably be of no help. You either know him or you don't. RBI double.

4. In 1976 he hit .033 but stole 20 bases for the A's; he left the majors in 1981 with 103 career stolen bases and just 36 hits. So what's the record he set? Well, how about for being the only man to appear in over 300 major league games and total three times as many stolen bases as he did hits? In any case, you're on tap for a rare home run on a player who was active in the past ten years.

5. He and Jerry Reuss are the only 200-game winners who never won 20 in a season. Got quite a bit of attention when he did it, but it's been awhile ago so I'll give a double.

6. He is the only 300-game winner who won 20 in a season just once. Single.

7. They are the only two batting-title winners since 1893 who also had seasons in which they were 20-game winners. One's easy and one's fairly tough, which is why you can get a triple for both but just a sac hit for being only half right.

8. In 1959 he collected a record-low 119 total bases in over 500 plate appearances. Huge hint: he might still one day make the Hall of Fame, by George, but not as a player. RBI double.

9. In 1906 he set an all-time bantam weight record when his 151 hits added up to only 162 total bases. Telling you he split the season between the Cardinals and the Giants will steer many away from a Phillies outfielder of that era who'd be a terrific guess. Adding that he led the NL in runs the following year should wipe any thought of it being a catcher out of your mind. Three-run homer.

10. He's the only hurler in big league history to win ten or more games over a two-year span without suffering a loss. Noting that two years before he started his

skein, he was 17–4 as a rookie and pitched against the Browns in the World Series should tell you plenty. Solo homer.

11. He is the only man in big league history to lead his league in steals as many as ten times. Not Brock or Cobb or George Case, and now I'll leave you alone to root out at max, an RBI single as best you can.

12. Among players with 400 or more attempted steals, his career efficiency ratio of .867 is easily the best in history. You'd have had to spend the last ten years in another galaxy to miss singling here.

13. The same season Rickey Henderson nailed a record 130 sacks, one of his teammates set an all-time single-season efficiency record when he nabbed 16 stolen bases without once being caught. Take two for this former utility infielder whose record was shattered in 1988 when Kevin McReynolds snared 21 bags uncaught.

14. During his career he achieved only 43 triples and stolen bases combined, easily the fewest among players in over 2,000 games. Have to be a lot faster than this slowfoot to stretch a hit here into a double.

15. He was a member of the 30/30 club (at least 30 steals and 30 homers in the same season) a record five times. Single.

16. What pitcher holds the record for the lowest winning percentage (.333) by an ERA leader and the lowest winning percentage (.333) by a strikeout leader? Your clue, if you really need it, is that he set both marks in the same season. Single for the man who got so little for doing so much; RBI for the year it happened.

SCORING CHART

Potential   At-Bats: 16
Total Bases: 34

                             Hits:

Potential
RBIS: 10   RBIS:

                             Total Bases:

41. Glorious Glovemen

1. He broke Gerry Priddy's major league record and
   his own NL record when he took part in 161 double
   plays in 1966. All you should need for a single.

2. This catcher broke his own major league mark, set in
   1914, when he bagged 238 assists in 1915. The clue
   that Edd Roush wasn't among the men he threw out
   stealing that year because Roush was a teammate
   won't help you half as much probably as my jogging
   your memory that there were three major leagues at
   the time. Two-run homer.

3. While we're on the subject, though, how many know
   who's the only catcher in 100+ games ever to *average*
   two assists per game in a season? He had 214 assists
   in 107 games and set a more familiar record 13 years
   later when he became the first man in this century to
   manage flag-winning teams in two different cities.
   With all that, how can you miss zapping a double?

4. Thanks largely to a record skein of 261 consecutive
   errorless chances, he set an all-time single-season mark
   for third sackers in 1974 with a .989 FA. Infield single.

5. After coming to the Red Sox from the Browns, this
   outfielder in 1926 played a record seven consecutive
   games (one which even went extra innings) without
   handling a single chance. This baby's tough enough
   for an RBI triple.

6. His 359 career errors are the most of any third baseman active after 1900. Clearly he played a long time,
but I'll still wager a two-run double a lot of you come
up empty here even knowing he and the "Chanceless"
outfielder were teammates for several seasons.

7. Only once has a third baseman ever handled over
600 chances, excluding errors, in a season. Knowing
that he also had 29 homers and 118 RBIs that year
and his name isn't Nettles should help you to a
stand-up double.

8. Like those third basemen, don't I? Well, I ain't done
yet. Homer by naming the hot cornerman who led
the NL in errors in 1892 with 78 and had an .882 FA,
but nevertheless set an NL record for the most assists
(382) that stood until _____ had 391 in 1966. Extra
ribby for correctly filling in the blank.

9. And next we got to the rookie who in 1953 handled
but 399 chances, including errors, making him the
first third sacker in history with fewer than 400 total
chances in 154 or more games. The tidbit that he was
also the first third sacker ever to collect 100 or more
RBIs in each of his first two seasons should lure you
to work hard enough here to score an RBI double.

10. And, yeah, there's one more. In 1971 this Indians
third sacker shattered all records when he partici-
pated in 54 double plays. Why's this only a single?
Well, I'm assuming you realize that anybody so good
could hardly have stayed in a Cleveland uniform very
long.

11. Talk about good, he holds the record for the most
years (4) with 500 or more outfield putouts and also
the record for the most years (9) with over 400.
Several Hall of Fame gardeners who were active
during his era got more ink for their gloves, but he
got far more balls and you're richer by an RBI single, I hope.

12. To end with a flurry of sharp singles, six in a row to be exact, identify first the shortstop who holds the record for being a league leader in FA the most times.

13. Now the second sacker who has the same record.

14. Ditto for the catcher.

15. And once again I'm caught in a lie. I think, on further consideration, that the outfielder who was an FA league leader the most times is hard enough to merit an RBI double.

SCORING CHART

Potential
Total Bases: 28   At-Bats: 15

                                   Hits:

Potential
RBIS: 10   RBIS:

                                   Total Bases:

42. Minor League Maestros

1. He broke in with Traverse City of the Michigan League in 1911 and finished in 1928 with Milwaukee, AA. But it was another AA club—Kansas City—that was the beneficiary of most of his slugging feats. The all-time AA home run leader, he also holds the circuit's single-season RBI record with 191 in 1921. A flop in several major league trials in the teens, he was active in Milwaukee amateur baseball circles until his death in 1963. Double.

2. In 1936 he hit .321 with 117 RBIs for Alexandria of the Evangeline League while teaming up with Dyna-mite Dunn, who that season hit an OB record five homers in a game. Five years later he set a Southern

Association record when he hit .414 for Nashville. In 1954, at 39, he led the Texas League with a .358 mark. His lone big league season as a full-time regular was his first, 1942, when he hit .292 for Cleveland and set an AL yearling record for a 154-game season by participating in 156 contests. Three-run triple.

3. He was the AL's leading hitter in 1900, the last year it was a minor league, and also led the loop in 1899, the last year it was known as the Western League. In 1901, at 35, he hit .320 for Washington and set a record for the highest batting average by a player in his final major league season. The reason he wasn't asked back in 1902 by the Senators is unfathomable now, but you can surely fathom why you're being asked to name him for a two-run double.

4. Notch a grand slam by identifying the Tigers utility infielder in the early '40s who shocked the baseball world in 1939 by hitting .439 for Beckley of the Mountain States League and posting a .790 slugging average, both of which are OB records for a shortstop.

5. In 1954 he had the most gigantic year since WW II of any player in the majors or high minors when he copped the Southern Association Triple Crown by rapping .345 with 64 homers and 161 RBIs. He struck out, literally, in several subsequent trials with the Giants, but for that one season this free-swinger struck gold. Run-scoring double.

6. The Cubs enjoyed this outfielder's services for several years before he played a record 18 seasons with Los Angeles of the PCL and collected more hits in OB (4,093) than anyone except Pete Rose, Ty Cobb, and Hank Aaron. Double.

7. When he led the Texas League in 1949 by hitting .355 for Oklahoma City, it was his third bat crown in three years. He shone in a brief trial with Cleveland the following season, but age—he was 29 by 1950

and had lost several years to WW II—kept back this big first sacker whose bat devastated the minors in the late '40s. Three-run homer.

8. Change of pace: a guy who was terrible in the minors. He hit .238 as a 19-year-old PCL rookie for San Francisco in 1940 and .216 in 1942. Ten years later this first sacker won his second of two successive AL bat crowns. RBI single.

9. In the same vein, here's another who did better in top company. In 1905, with San Francisco of the PCL, this shortstop hit .159 in 215 games and made 98 errors. Two years earlier, with Cleveland, he also made 98 errors—but he hit .185. I said better, remember; I didn't say he did well. Four-run homer.

10. This trio formed the heart of the Fort Worth mound corps from 1920–25 when the Cats were streaking to six consecutive Texas League pennants. Each pitched in the majors, albeit briefly, and all were with Fort Worth for 11 seasons. The clues that one holds the TL record for career wins, another was 9–0 as a rookie with the 1926 A's and the third later pitched in the PCL still make you a dark horse to score all three for a three-run homer. Take a triple for knowing two of them and a single for just one.

11. Nearly 32 years old before he played his first full season in pro ball, he finished in 1945 at age 46 with the IL record for career home runs (258), all of which were hit while playing for Buffalo. Denizens of that cold town nab an easy two-bagger; the rest of you may have to hustle.

12. In 1913 he won 21 games for the White Sox and tied a rookie record with eight shutouts. Five years later, when his wing went, the Sox gave up on him, but he resurfaced in 1922 with the Pirates as an outfielder and hit .368 with 75 RBIs in just 220 at-bats. Deeming him too old at 34 a year later, the Pirates cut

him, so he went to Columbus for several fine seasons and then on to Indianapolis, where he led the AA in batting in 1927 with a .385 mark. The prototype of the many outstanding pitchers who became great hitters when their arms faltered, he'd rebel if I awarded more than a two-run double for him after clueing you in on his rookie mark.

13. The Phils cut this frosh after the 1921 season and gave their second-base post to Frank Parkinson. Parkie had one decent year before slipping badly, but our man proceeded to deck Coast League pitchers for nearly a decade. Considered the PCL's all-time best second baseman by many observers, he was runner-up for the loop bat crown in 1931 after hitting .350 with 28 homers for the Mission Reds a year earlier. Three-run homer.

14. He led the PCL in homers for three straight years (1955–57) and copped a record three straight MVP Awards. The highpoint of his career came in 1956 when he won a PCL Triple Crown; the bottom was reached four years later when he hit .207 for the Tigers while platooning at first base with Norm Cash. He also failed earlier with the Cards, Cubs, and Dodgers before achieving mild success with the expansion Angels. Two bases for this huge slugger who was atypical of the many minor league stars of his time in that he was given every chance in the majors.

15. Another who got more major league opportunities than a cat has lives, this lefty first sacker used the second of his two IL Triple Crowns, in 1958 at age 34, to goad the Pirates into granting him one last shot. And lo and behold, he made good finally by staying around Pittsburgh for three full seasons, long enough to get in sufficient time to collect a pension from the game. Considered the premier player in the minors in the '50s. RBI single.

SCORING CHART

Potential
Total Bases: 39

Potential
RBIS: 27

At-Bats: 15

Hits:

RBIS:

Total Bases:

October

Forgotten Series Hero

We all know that Kurt Gibson's last-gasp homer in the 1988 World Series was the first circuit clout in the fall classic's history to give a trailing team a victory with two out in the bottom of the ninth. I'll wager an RBI two-bagger, though, that you'll be stumped when called on to name the only player ever to win *two* games in the same Series with a late-inning home run.

His first came in the top of the ninth inning of the Series opener. A surprise outfield starter after age and injuries had reduced him to part-time status for most of the regular season, he came to the plate with the score tied 4–4, hit a line drive between Bob Meusel and Whitey Witt, and legged it out for the only game-winning inside-the-park homer in Series history.

Two days later, in Game Three, playing in front of the largest crowd to watch a baseball game anywhere up to that time, he poled a four-bagger into the rightfield bleachers off Sam Jones in the seventh inning for the only run of the contest.

His unanticipated heroics notwithstanding, his team, unlike Gibson's, dropped the next three games and the Series to a favored American League club that it had swept the previous fall. Credit an extra RBI if you also know the two teams involved in this classic matchup *and* the year it occurred.

Need another clue? Okay, both of our man's home runs came in the same park, but one was made in the top half of an inning and the other in the bottom half of one. How could that be? It's easy, if you know your history.

43. October Heroes

1. Prior to his death in 1972 he was the last surviving participant in the first modern World Series. In it he scored eight runs for the winning team and had three triples. Enough clues here for experts to find the answer fairly apparent. Three-bagger.

2. In 1951, his first pro year, he was 21–3 for Hazard of the Mountain States League; four years later he did something in a World Series that was never done before or after. Need both him and what he did for an RBI single.

3. His three saves, two of them in the sixth and seventh games, helped his team to become the second in the franchise's history to win a World Series after trailing 3 games to 1. Double, plus an RBI for the team and year.

4. He was the last player-manager to win a World Championship with an NL team. Won't come to you in a flash, but with some thought you can't miss scoring an RBI single.

5. He won the playoff game that gave his team the pennant, then won his team's first home Series victory in 28 years, and saved his team's last Series triumph to date. Some will find him harder than the team, so it's a single for the team and two RBIs for him.

6. His team played in one World Series and one League Championship Series during his 22-year career in its uniform. Although not a regular during either season, he played every game in the outfield in both fall series. Single.

7. He would have been the only 35-game winner to pitch in a World Series if his manager and owner had

not refused to play a championship series in fear that their crosstown rivals would cop the AL flag. He's worth a single; his team and the year he missed out go for an RBI apiece.

8. He pitched three consecutive complete-game victories to bring his team the title in the first World Series in history played to a conclusion. One for him; an RBI apiece for the team and year we're talking about.

9. His team won a five-game Series with a 10-run seventh inning in Game Four to overcome an 8–0 deficit and with three runs in the bottom of the ninth inning in Game Five to overcome a 2–0 deficit; in each game his homer with men aboard provided the comeback spark. Solo homer, plus an RBI for the team and year. Single if you miss him but know the team and year.

10. This rookie righthander ruined Cobb's last bid to play for a World Champion when he notched three Series wins, including an 8–0 shutout in Game Seven. Two-bagger for him; RBI for his team and year of glory. Zippo, though, if you stumble on him.

11. He set a record when he bagged eight RBIs in each of two consecutive Series and totaled seven homers, three of them coming consecutively in the game that brought his team its first World Championship in 15 years. Got to have the whole bundle—him, his team, the year it broke through—for a mere single.

12. This keystone combo was the only two regulars to hit .300 in both the LCS and the WS for the first team south of Shreveport to cop a pennant. Have to know a little geography and about the same amount about baseball to nail an RBI single here.

13. He led all hitters in the 1980 Series with four homers while hitting .400 with eight RBIs; moreover, in the

course of it he collected his only triple of the season and the first in his three-year career. You were there for it, most of you, in your living rooms anyway. Yet a double says this one'll slip by you.

14. He was the lone Yankees pitcher to collect a win in all four series during the club's record World Championship string from 1936–39. Triple.

15. They are the only two managers since 1908 who faced each other in consecutive World Series while not at the helm of a New York-based team. Need 'em both and the years it happened to score an RBI double.

SCORING CHART

Potential Total Bases: 26	At-Bats: 15
	Hits:
Potential RBIS: 14	RBIS:
	Total Bases:

44. Their Niche Is Secure

1. At one point in his career he had the highest single-season batting average since 1900 for four different teams. He still holds three 20th-century club records for the top single-season batting average. His name merits just a single, but knowing all four clubs whose team records he once held gets two RBIs as long as you correctly identify the three franchises whose records he still holds.

2. He holds both the record for the highest winning percentage by a 300-game winner and the highest career winning percentage by a pitcher involved in over 400 decisions, major league and minor league stats inclusive. Merely a single.

3. In 1931 he set the White Sox all-time single-season record for the most times reached base safely on hits, walks, and hit by pitches (309). Home run.

4. He holds the NL record for the most times reached base safely on hits, walks, and hit by pitches—334 in 1929 with the Phillies. RBI single.

5. The all-time Giants' franchise record for the most times reached base safely is 314, set in 1950 by a player who collected just 158 hits that season. Enough info there for the shrewd to bag a snap RBI double.

6. His 27 wins in 1939 made him the co-holder of the modern record for the most wins in a season by a Cinci pitcher. Two-bagger.

7. He holds the Baltimore club record for the most wins in a season with a total that is only two short of _____'s all-time franchise record, set in 1922. For a single, name the O's record holder; take an RBI for knowing the year he set the mark; make it a two-run homer if, in addition, you zap the franchise record holder and the number of wins he had in '22.

8. Who was the first pitcher to win 100 games in each league in this century? RBI bunt single.

9. He holds the modern record for the most wins in a season by a pitcher on a club that finished below second place in its league. Single for him alone; two ribbies for also knowing his team, the year he did it, and the number of victories he had.

10. This Hall of Famer set an all-time bantam-weight record in 1922 when he failed to homer in 672 at-bats. The clue that he also is the lone Hall of Famer who was banished to the minors in mid-career should hurry even you tortoises in for a double ahead of the throw.

11. In 1904 this pair helped usher in the deadball era when they hit .207 and .189, the lowest averages ever for a second baseman and a shortstop respectively in 500 or more at-bats. The second sacker, who years earlier had been the first to accomplish a rare slugging feat, played for the Tigers; his weak-hitting counterpart played beside a third sacker, not related to him, who had the same last name. Two-run triple for both men and a third RBI for knowing the second sacker's slugging feat; single if you score on just one.

12. Among pitchers with 250 or more decisions who were never on a pennant winner, his .626 career winning percentage is easily the highest. This luckless Hall of Famer's worth an RBI single.

13. At the conclusion of the season in which he netted his 200th win, he had an incredible .720 career winning percentage (216–84). Single for him, plus an RBI for the year he claimed No. 200.

14. He broke Ted Williams's "graybeard" record of 29 homers when he slammed 34 four-baggers in 1987, the season in which he turned 40. Single.

15. He set an all-time record for third sackers when he collected 145 RBIs in the same season a soph slugger was setting the NL RBI mark for third basemen. The 145-RBI man's a single; RBI for the NL record setter; and a second RBI for the year both soared.

SCORING CHART

Potential Total Bases: 25	At-Bats: 15
	Hits:
Potential RBIS: 17	RBIS:
	Total Bases:

45. October Heroes

1. He was the first member of the Yankees to play in a
   World Series at the position that would subsequently
   feature Earl Combs, Joe DiMaggio, and Mickey Mantle. This's guaranteed to leave some of you feeling
   witless when you see the answer. Three-run homer.

2. This catcher was the first player to homer in a Series
   game played west of Hannibal, Mo. Tougher than
   your last geography exercise, so I'll give a two-run
   double.

3. Appearing in four games of a five-game Series, he
   had a perfect 0.00 ERA and in Game Four collected his team's lone win with the aid of Lee May's
   three-run homer. Clues are right to make an expert
   sing all the way to a triple, plus an RBI for the year
   at issue.

4. In the process of bagging his record tenth Series win
   he saw his WS shutout-skein mark broken in the
   second inning of the lid lifter between two teams that
   had once occupied the same park but now played in
   cities 3,000 miles apart. Single for him; RBI for the
   enemy team.

5. He was the last Cubs pitcher both to win and lose a
   Series game. Really, all you have to know is who
   started the seventh game blowout that marked the
   Bruins' last fall appearance. One-run double.

6. He's remembered now for just one thing, and this is
   it: his complete-game shutout in Game Seven wrapped
   up the 1956 World Series. RBI triple.

7. His niche in history is secure as the first major leaguer to enter the armed services in WW I and the
   leading hitter in the only Series won by an NL team
   based in Boston. Two-bagger.

8. They are the only two players to participate as losers in every post-season series that featured a team from Anaheim. Need both for an RBI single; sac hit for scoring on just one.

9. This Cy Young winner worked only one contest in the World Series, a 5–4 complete-game win, after starting a record four playoff games. He's a single; the year he did it gets an RBI.

10. He won his first big league game with Detroit in 1916 after posting a 31–7 record for Syracuse in the New York State League; his last win came in a World Series 13 years later when he set a new single-game strikeout record. The Syracuse clue's there just to assure you this guy was a pretty good pitcher, no one-game fluke he, which is why you're only up for a double.

11. In the first modern World Series he led all hitters in both batting and slugging and also hit the first modern WS homer—all in a losing cause. If you don't happen to know this, move along. All the mulling in the world won't see you bring his name out of some dark catacomb in your memory bank. Two-run triple.

12. His victory in relief—which was only his second win of the season and his last in the uniform he'd worn for ten years— wrapped up the title for the last team to win three consecutive World Championships. Again, either shoot the moon on a quick guess and hope to get lucky or else move along. Double.

13. His team shattered the record in its league for the most wins in a season, but he was its lone bright spot in the Series, hitting .500 and nearly winning Game One with a 440-foot shot that was caught by a Hall of Famer with his back to the plate. One base for him; RBI for the Famer who robbed him.

14. This MVP winner's first start of the season narrowly missed becoming the first home game in Series history won by his team when he lost 1–0 on a sac fly by Jerry Coleman. He's a double; the year rates an RBI.

15. Of all the LCS's that have gone the limit, whether it be five or seven games, only one was decided by a home run on the final pitch of the final game. For two bases, who hit the pennant-winning gamer? Collect an RBI for the year and two more ribbies if you know what pitcher he victimized.

SCORING CHART

Potential Total Bases: 31	At-Bats: 15
	Hits:
Potential RBIS: 18	RBIS:
	Total Bases:

46. North of the Border

1. More than 100 years after he did it, he still remains the lone Triple Crown winner to have been born in Canada. Died there, too, of a heart attack, in 1915. Double.

2. A native of Ontario, he made perhaps the blackest big league debut ever in 1912 when he hit .122 in 196 at-bats as a shortstop for the Braves. After a long apprenticeship in the minors, he rebounded with the Senators in 1920 and was still a major league regular a decade later. Two-run triple.

3. This lefty outfielder from Ontario hit .312 for the 1890 Cincinnati Reds in his only full big league season after burning up the top Canadian leagues, then

quietly starred for nearly a decade in the high minors without ever getting another chance up top. Solo homer.

4. Short on quality but long on oddities, the 1962 Mets employed two Canadian-born relievers. Name either one for a double; homer for both.

5. This Montreal native spent nearly a decade in the lower minors before hitting the majors with the wartime Boston Braves. The following year, 1945, he played in his hometown and led the International League in hits, doubles, and triples before jumping to the Mexican League. Upon his return from south of the border, he starred in the Provincial League, one of the few circuits that refused to recognize the OB blacklist against the jumpers. RBI triple.

6. In 1980 this 20-year-old outfielder became the first Toronto Blue Jay who was born in Montreal. You had to be quick, though, to catch his act because he lasted just a few weeks. Two-run homer.

7. The first player in AL history to collect 40 doubles, 20 triples, and 20 homers in the same season was a Canadian having his first really big season since he'd rapped .340 three years earlier as a rookie teammate of Bob Feller's. RBI double.

8. Never much as a player, this Nova Scotia native managed both the Red Sox and the Braves during the deadball era. Hit this one in the drink and collect four bases.

9. His name alone, when pronounced correctly, told you that he was probably French Canadian. If I add that his best years were with Houston and that in 1970 he set an Expos' record for saves (23), since broken, can you claim a one-run double?

10. Quick now, what was the first season that both Canadian-based major league teams finished above .500? Single.

11. This lefty from Rebecca, Ontario, didn't make the majors until 1941 when he was 33; he stayed, however, until he was past 40, dividing his time about equally with the Red Sox and Phillies and earning kudos as one of the best hitting pitchers of his era. Solo homer.

12. Nicknamed Frenchy though he was born in the states, he won fame in the majors for his mustache and his pinch-hitting prowess—he hit a phenomenal .465 in that role for the Cards in 1938—and copped the Canadian-American League batting title when he hit .363 in 1946 as a player-manager for Three Rivers. Taking that job cost him dearly, however, as it terminated his major league career after the 1945 season and deprived him of the pension he would have received if he'd played even a single game up top in 1946, the year the plan started. RBI single.

13. The very first recognized minor league champions were a Canadian team in the International Association back in 1877. Wager a three-run homer you can't name that club.

SCORING CHART

Potential Total Bases: 38	At-Bats: 13
	Hits:
Potential RBIS: 15	RBIS:
	Total Bases:

47. Great Goats and Victims

1. These two players each hold an unwelcome and unparalleled distinction; one lined into the only unassisted triple play in World Series history, and the other took a disputed called third strike to ring down the curtain on the only perfect game in Series history. Learning they both were lefties, both were skilled pinch hitters who played for the same team, and both had the same last name should make this a cinch RBI double— so long as you get both of their first names, of course.

2. He served up Pete Rose's 4,192nd hit. Betting a double a lot of you haven't yet entered this morsel in your computer memories.

3. Pitching for the St. Louis Maroons in 1886, this righthander, who only two years earlier had been the most promising young hurler in baseball, was victimized for a record seven home runs in a game by Detroit; upon leaving the majors the following season, he spent most of the rest of his life in San Quentin on a manslaughter conviction. Two-bagger.

4. He made three World Series starts, completed them all, and posted a dazzling 0.89 ERA in fall play, yet came away with only one win. One of his defeats was a 14-inning 2–1 loss in 1916 to Babe Ruth in the longest game in Series history. The final clue that he had one of the best pickoff moves ever should aid you to pick off an RBI double.

5. Probably the leading victim of the increased mound distance, after *averaging* 41 wins over the previous three seasons before 10½ feet were added to the distance he had to hurl, he won only 44 more games in the majors. One-run single.

6. No pitcher in this century has ever lost 20 games while winning fewer than three. He came the closest of any since 1916 when he was 2–19 for the 1986 Pirates. Single.

7. Cookie Lavagetto's ninth-inning two-out double robbed him of a World Series no-hitter. The final rub: he never again started a game in the majors. Double.

8. Sent to the Braves by the Cubs, he posted a 5.30 ERA in 165 innings in 1911, the highest by an ERA qualifier during the deadball era; later, though, he found solace for several seasons with New Orleans of the Southern Association. Yeah, I'll agree this merits a grand slam homer.

9. What southpaw, who led the AL in strikeouts his first two seasons and was coming off a 20-win campaign in 1956, had his career all but ended when his cheekbone was shattered by a line drive early in the 1957 season? Single for him; two ribbies for the man who hit the screamer back through the box.

10. His mates called him Smiley, but he had little to smile about in his four-year career. He exited in 1982 with no career wins and 16 losses, the most ever among pitchers who failed to record at least one victory in the majors. Forgotten him already? Two bases if you haven't.

11. This Pirates second sacker in 1935 became the first pitcher in the 20th century to go down on strikes five times in a single game. True, you may not be old enough to have seen him play, but you're not too young to have seen his name in all the record books. Triple.

12. What Hall of Fame backstopper was the victim when Pepper Martin swiped five bases and the Cardinals

eight altogether to his team's none in the 1931 World Series? Easy single, and an alert not to feel too cocky.

13. Because this next one's a dilly. Claude Willoughby was spared the ignominy of having the worst ERA of any pitcher in this century in 150+ innings when what teammate of his on the 1930 Phillies posted a 7.71 ERA to his 7.59? Two-run homer.

14. Jack Nabors and Tom Sheehan had a combined 2–35 record for the 1916 A's—the worst AL team ever with a .235 winning percentage. What two pitchers between them accounted for 29 of the A's 36 wins? Three-run homer for both; double for one.

15. Long the Red Sox regular shortstop, he lost his job in 1915 and had to move to second base. During the transition, to add insult, he was appointed the first road roommate of a madcap rookie named Babe Ruth. Solo homer.

SCORING CHART

Potential Total Bases: 35	At-Bats: 15
	Hits:
Potential RBIS: 15	RBIS:
	Total Bases:

48. Death in the Afternoon

1. Bright's Disease took the life of what Giants Hall of Famer in 1927, just months after he turned 30? Rates a single.

2. A 19-game winner in 1928 as a rookie with the last-place Red Sox, he was murdered during spring training four years later near Century, Florida. Homer.

3. McGraw tired of this pitcher's escapades and gave him what amounted to a permanent suspension from the Giants in 1911; the following September he was found dead in bed of a brain concussion sustained in a brawl at a sandlot game. Homer.

4. Just beginning to find his batting eye after a shaky frosh season, this Red Sox first sacker and former college football All-American was hospitalized early in the 1955 campaign and died while there of a pulmonary embolism. RBI double.

5. On the comeback trail, this ex-Cardinals' spit-baller was 21–9 as the player-manager for Houston of the Texas League in 1925 before he was killed in a private plane crash after the season's close. Two-run homer.

6. For reasons that will probably always remain a mystery, this star outfielder committed suicide in spring training prior to the 1907 season while serving as the Red Sox player-manager. RBI double.

7. A bad heart forced this pitcher to quit after he was 18–6 with the 1927 Yankees and killed him before the following year was out. Take another two-bagger.

8. This 30-year-old rookie seemed to fill the Cubs' third-base hole when he hit .282 in 1911 and had 19 steals. Over the winter, however, he succumbed to a ruptured appendix. Have to give a grand slam here.

9. The most ill-fated minor league team in history, Portsmouth, the 1915 champions of the Ohio State League, had three young stars who would soon make the majors. One, Ralph Sharman, the 1917 Texas League batting champ, perished in the 1918 flu epidemic; a

second, Pickles Dillhoefer, died early in 1922 of typhoid fever following surgery. Later in 1922 the third star of the Portsmouth club died of a brain tumor after hitting .350 for the Cardinals the previous season. Would have asked you to name all three men, but this one's too depressing to spend any more time on than it should take you to net a two-run double for the Cardinal gardener.

10. And you can make a quick exit here altogether just as soon as you identify the only 3,000-hit man to die while still an active player. One-base hit.

SCORING CHART

Potential Total Bases: 26	At-Bats: 10
	Hits:
Potential RBIS: 12	RBIS:
	Total Bases:

49. October Heroes

1. He batted .414, stole seven bases, made 12 hits, and scored eight runs, but saw a teammate, who played in only three of the seven games, cop the Series MVP award. By properly analyzing the clues you should be a lock to score both him and his teammate for an RBI double.

2. This shortstop's nine hits and .500 average led all batters in the Series that pitted the Murderer's Row against the Waner brothers. Triple.

3. He is the lone NL pitcher since 1920 to win three complete-game victories seven-game Series without pitching the Series opener. Two-run double.

4. Can the same be said about an AL pitcher? You bet it can. Moreover, in his first Series at-bat he hit his first and only home run in the majors. That clue knocks it down to an RBI single.

5. After bringing his team back from the dead with a ninth-inning homer in the fifth game of an LCS, he seemingly clinched the WS with an overtime four-bagger in Game Six—only to watch helplessly while his team frittered away victory in the bottom of the inning. How quickly we forget, the few of us who need longer than three seconds to single here.

6. In the last World Series between the NL and the AA, what batting-crown winner of that season led his underdog team to a six-game tie? RBI triple.

7. Lombardi's injury and Hershberger's suicide forced the Reds to use this 40-year-old backstopper in the 1940 Series. All he did was hit .353 and swipe the only base that was pilfered that fall. Solo homer.

8. The first pitcher to appear in every winning game for a World Champion, he posted two victories and two saves and won the MVP car. Big clue: what you've got going here is the first Series in history that didn't have a complete game by a pitcher on *either* side. Two-run double.

9. In the 1975 Series, considered by many to be the most exciting ever, he took the loss in the crucial seventh game and never again figured in a decision in the majors. Two-run homer.

10. His grand slam homer led an 18-run barrage that brought his team a crushing win in Game Two of the 1936 Series after its opponents had broken its record streak of 12 consecutive Series wins in the opener. Okay, he's a double, and there are two RBIs at stake if you nail the pitcher who stymied his club in the Series lid lifter.

11. He became the only pitcher to record four decisions in a six-game Series while leading his team to the last World Championship won by a franchise based in the nation's second largest city. Two for him; RBI for the year he did it.

12. His lone Series appearance was in an all-important seventh game when his manager named him his club's starter and then relieved him with a lefty after he faced just two batters to foil the rival manager who'd stacked his lineup with lefty hitters. Homer for him, RBI for the southpaw who relieved him and an RBI for each of the managers involved. Hey, that's a grand slam, but it's down to just a double if you know only the managers.

13. His home run early in Game One was the only RBI his team made during the *entire* Series via a base hit. Bingle for the team and year; up to a four-bagger if you know him too.

14. He surrendered 13 hits and saw his mates make two errors behind him, but won 8–1 in a Series game that featured the first Series grand slam, the only Series triple play, and the first Series homer hit by a pitcher, none other than our man under consideration. Bag a two-bagger for him; a ribby for the guy who hit the grand slam; another ribby for the guy who engineered the triple play.

15. Selected his league's MVP in the only year a team swept both an LCS and a WS, he took part in every post-season game his club played that season. Sounds like a fairly easy RBI single, and it can be. But fair warning: you get a blank if you come up half empty on this one.

SCORING CHART

Potential
Total Bases: 37

Potential
RBIS: 21

At-Bats: 15

Hits:

RBIS:

Total Bases:

Answers

APRIL

Opening Day Classic
Pop Dillon, Hugh Duffy, Roscoe Miller.

1. Fabled Freshmen

1. Dwight Gooden
2. Fernando Valenzuela
3. Alex Kellner, 1949
4. George Stone
5. Alvin Davis
6. Hal Trosky
7. Jimmy Williams
8. Albie Pearson
9. Willie McCovey, Pacific Coast League
10. George Watkins, 1930
11. Joe Charboneau
12. Tom Seaver
13. Dale Alexander, 1929
14. Mitch Williams, Texas Rangers
15. 1903 Dodgers, Henry Schmidt and Oscar Jones
16. Cuckoo Christensen

2. Moments to Remember

1. Joe Gordon
2. Bob Allen
3. Jack Scott
4. Ken Johnson
5. Rickey Henderson
6. Bob Elliott, third base
7. Willie Stargell, 1979
8. Jim O'Rourke
9. Mel Ott
10. Ted Williams, 1949, George Kell
11. Bob Horner
12. Eddie Ainsmith
13. Bill Sayles
14. Vic Raschi

3. Glorious Glovemen

1. Bill Freehan
2. Eddie Miller
3. Heinie Groh and Willie Kamm
4. Pete Alexander
5. Johnny Roseboro
6. Ray Mueller in 1944
7. Johnny Edwards
8. Tris Speaker
9. Chuck Klein
10. Sam Rice
11. Gene Woodling, 1951–53
12. Bid McPhee
13. Heinie Groh, third base
14. Charlie Grimm
15. Ferris Fain

4. Death in the Afternoon

1. Ray Chapman
2. John Dodge
3. Ken Hubbs
4. Jake Daubert
5. Hub Collins
6. King Cole
7. Lyman Bostock
8. Walt Lerian
9. Jim Umbricht
10. Thurman Munson

5. Team Teasers

1. Cubs
2. Indians, Alvin Dark
3. Reds, 1975
4. Pirates, 1902, Jack Chesbro
5. Cardinals, 1911, Helen Britton
6. Louisville, 1889–90
7. 1973 Braves, Hank Aaron, Davy Johnson, and Darrell Evans
8. Angels, 1962
9. Giants
10. Jim Presley and Danny Tartabull, Mariners
11. Kansas City A's, Ned Garver
12. Brooklyn Atlantics, Charlie Sweasy
13. Brewers
14. Baltimore Orioles, International League, Jack Dunn
15. Yankees, Clark Griffith

6. Black Is Beautiful

1. Frank Robinson
2. Joe Black
3. Charlie Morton, 1884 Toledo Blue Stockings, Fleet and Welday Walker
4. Bud Fowler
5. Artie Wilson
6. Brooks Lawrence
7. First base, Vic Power, 1956
8. Third base
9. Don Newcombe
10. Newk again, and for shame if you took the bait and went for Sam "Toothpick" Jones
11. Cecil Cooper
12. Maury Wills
13. National League, 1960
14. Browns-Orioles, Bob Boyd
15. Willie Horton

7. Their Niche Is Secure

1. Sam Thompson
2. Sam Crawford
3. Pete Rose
4. Fritz Peterson
5. Tommy Byrne
6. Amos Rusie
7. Spud Chandler
8. Jack Chesbro
9. Bert Campaneris
10. Willie Mays
11. Pete Rose
12. Lou Gehrig
13. Mike Marshall
14. Jack Quinn
15. Rocky Colavito, 1965

MAY

Southpaw Surprise
Ron Guidry, Billy Martin
8. Moments to Remember

1. Frank Tanana
2. Mel Ott
3. Roy Face
4. Al Zarilla
5. Phil Niekro, Early Wynn, and Gaylord Perry
6. George Uhle, Cleveland
7. Erv Kantlehner
8. Fred Odwell
9. Tommy Holmes, 1945
10. Bert Cunningham
11. Preacher Roe
12. Bob Veale, Pirates
13. It was the first time in 2,131 games played by the Yankees that Lou Gehrig's name wasn't in the box score.
14. Fire Trucks, Eddie Yost

9. Great Goats and Victims

1. Al Downing
2. Bob Moose
3. Vince DiMaggio
4. Al Bridwell
5. Jim McAndrew
6. Don Newcombe
7. Jimmy O'Connell
8. Ray Fisher
9. Johnny Pesky, Harry Walker
10. Mike Parrott
11. Ross Barnes
12. Reggie Jackson, 1983
13. Sam Gibson
14. George Mullin
15. Hugh Casey

10. South of the Border

1. Esteban Bellan
2. Dolph Luque
3. Alex and Chico Carrasquel
4. Hector Espino
5. Jose, Hector, and Cirilio Cruz
6. Roberto Clemente, 1961
7. Mike Gonzalez
8. Joe Azcue
9. Juan Marichal
10. Roger Moret
11. Julio Javier
12. Pete Ramos
13. Diomedes and Chi Chi Olivo
14. Willie Hernandez
15. Pedro "Tony" Oliva

11. Minor League Maestros

1. George Whiteman
2. "Prince" Henry Oana
3. Dud Lee
4. Joe Hauser
5. Paul Strand
6. Al Pinkston
7. Kid Mohler
8. Yam Yaryan
9. Irv Waldron
10. Frank Shellenback
11. Roy "Tex" Sanner
12. Tony Frietas
13. Steve Dalkowski
14. Joe Wilhoit
15. Perry Werden

12. Super Siblings

1. Gaylord and Jim Perry
2. Phil and Joe Niekro
3. Paul and Dizzy Dean, the Gas House Gang —the 1934 Cardinals
4. Jesse and Virgil Barnes, 1927
5. Fred and Josh Clarke
6. Lee and Jesse Tannehill
7. Doc and Jimmy Johnston, Cleveland and Brooklyn
8. Paul and Lloyd Waner
9. Ike and Danny Boone
10. Tony and Billy Conigliaro
11. Gene and George Freese
12. Hank and Tommy Aaron
13. Rick, Wes, and George Ferrell
14. Mike and Matt Kilroy
15. Zach and Mack Wheat

13. Their Niche Is Secure

1. Ron Hunt, Don Baylor
2. Joe Adcock, Ebbets Field
3. Guy Hecker
4. Frank Chance and Bill Carrigan
5. John Crooks
6. Carl Hubbell and Harry Brecheen
7. Jim Palmer
8. Eddie Rommel
9. Buck Freeman
10. Pete Richert
11. Pete Alexander, Herb Score
12. His own, set in 1970
13. Cannonball Morris
14. Babe Ruth
15. John Tudor, 1985

14. Whatever Happened to . . . ?

1. Frank Robinson
2. Billy Sunday
3. Charlie Comiskey
4. Danny Ainger
5. Lee Richmond
6. Ted Lewis
7. Frank Fennelly
8. Ken Strong
9. Bill Lange
10. Chuck Connors and Johnny Berardino, *The Rifleman* and *General Hospital*
11. Sam Crane
12. George Halas
13. Dory Dean
14. Tim McCarver
15. Bobby Brown

JUNE

Leader of the Pack
Rod Carew, 1977, .388.
15. Team Teasers

1. 1939 Yankees, Browns
2. Giants, 1971, George Foster, Gaylord Perry, and Sam McDowell
3. Lefty Grove, A's
4. Cubs, Hank Sauer, Ernie Banks, and Andre Dawson
5. Giants, 1922–24
6. Cardinals, 1920, Robison Field
7. Cincinnati, Crosley Field, 1970
8. Polo Grounds, Giants, Yankees, and Mets
9. Phillies, Shibe Park, 1952
10. Louisville Redbirds
11. Ty Cobb; he never had a uniform number.
12. White Sox, Red Faber.
13. Phillies, Robin Roberts, 1952, and Steve Carlton, 1972
14. New York and Philadelphia
15. St. Louis Browns
16. Cardinals, 1987

16. Now batting for . . .

1. Yogi Berra
2. Ira Thomas in 1910
3. Smokey Burgess
4. Duke Farrell
5. Jose Morales
6. Joe Cronin
7. Sammy Hale
8. Candy Maldonado
9. Del Unser
10. Doc Miller
11. Sam Leslie
12. Al Kaline
13. Chick Outen and Frank Gibson
14. Mike O'Neill
15. Ed Coleman and Ray Pepper

17. Moments to Remember

1. Zoilo Versalles
2. Bob Lemon
3. Joe Jackson
4. Curt Flood, Senators
5. Ezra Sutton
6. Rogers Hornsby, 1926
7. Leon Viau
8. Mickey Mantle
9. Red Schoendienst
10. Gus Dorner
11. Bob Friend, Pirates
12. Ned Garber
13. One Arm Daily
14. Harry Anderson
15. Steve Carlton

18. Glorious Glovemen

1. Brooks Robinson
2. Randy Hundley
3. Brian Downing, 1982 and 1984
4. Phil Niekro
5. Bill Buckner
6. Bill Dahlen
7. Chet Lemon
8. Johnny Lush
9. Frankie Frisch
10. Lou Bierbauer, Pirates
11. Ed Hahn
12. Taylor Douthit
13. Ed Walsh
14. Tommy Holmes
15. Butch Hobson

19. Like Father Like Son

1. George, Dave, and Dick Sisler
2. Max and Hal Lanier
3. Lew Krause, Sr., and Jr.
4. Lee and Pat Riley
5. Danny and Jose Tartabull
6. Sam, Jerry, and John Hairston
7. Peaches and Jack Graham
8. Bob and Terry Kennedy
9. Mike and Tom Tresh
10. Jim Poole
11. Billy Sullivan, Sr., and Jr.
12. Harl Maggert and son Harl
13. Earle Mack, son of Connie Mack
14. Bobby and Barry Bonds
15. Gus and Buddy Bell

20. World War II Wrinkles

1. No, not Ducky
   Medwick, Mel Ott
2. Johnny Pesky
3. Nick Etten
4. George Caster
5. Dizzy Trout
6. Arky Vaughan
7. Jimmy Wasdell
8. Johnny Barrett
9. Hal Trosky
10. Eddie Busch
11. Billy Johnson
12. Snuffy Stirnweiss

21. Their Niche Is Secure

1. Sandy Koufax
2. Don Larsen
3. Kid Nichols
4. Gary Templeton
5. Dick Higham, 1882
6. Owen Wilson, 36 triples, 1912
7. Vern Stephens
8. Ernie Banks
9. Tony Fernandez
10. Warren Spahn
11. Steve Carlton
12. Charlie Gehringer
13. Killebrew and Kiner
14. Ted Williams
15. Hy Myers

JULY

Rapid Robert's Redux
Hal Newhouser
22. Moments to Remember

1. Tommy Herr, 1950
2. Wade Boggs, Heinie
   Manush, 241, 1928
3. John Clarkson, Giants
4. Willie Mays, 1965;
   George Foster, 1977
5. Charlie Robertson
6. Xavier Rescigno in 1944
   led NL in relief wins.
7. Willie Keeler, 1897
8. Atley Donald
9. Matty Alou
10. Erv Beck
11. Dave Koslo
12. Charlie Hodnett
13. Ben Cantwell
14. Jimmie Foxx
15. Mike Witt

23. North of the Border

1. Terry Puhl
2. Fergie Jenkins
3. Bill Phillips
4. Jacques Fournier
5. Pop Smith
6. Gus Dugas
7. Glenn Gorbus
8. Nig Clarke
9. John and Art Irwin
10. George Gibson
11. Jack Graney
12. Charlie Mead
13. Joe Yeager, Montreal, 1904

24. Super Siblings

1. Delahanty, Jim and Frank
2. Milt and Alex Gaston
3. Stan and Harry Coveleski
4. Bob and Ken Forsch, 1978 and 1979 (Bob threw another in 1983.)
5. Greg and Mike Maddux
6. Larry and Mike Corcoran
7. Frank and Joe Torre
8. The Alous
9. Herman and Harry Layne
10. Ken and George Brett
11. Joe, Vince, and Dom DiMaggio
12. Bob and Emil "Irish" Meusel
13. Joe and Luke Sewell
14. Ken and Clete Boyer
15. Lee and Carlos May

25. Great Goats and Victims

1. Willie McCovey
2. Larry French
3. Sudden Sam McDowell
4. George Scott
5. Larry McKeon
6. Babe Ruth
7. Mike Torrez
8. Dizzy Dean
9. Willie Davis
10. Chief Bender
11. Tracy Stallard
12. Ralph Branca, Bobby Thomson
13. Charlie Root
14. Jack Warhop
15. Roger Craig, Al Jackson, Jack Fisher, and, that perennial victim, Tracy Stallard

26. Forget Me Not

1. Lave Cross
2. Vic Willis
3. Pete Browning
4. Wade Boggs and Bill Madlock
5. Ed Konetchy
6. Dom DiMaggio
7. Deacon White
8. George Uhle
9. Jim Scott
10. Wilbur Cooper
11. George Davis
12. Cesar Tovar
13. Cal McVey
14. John Titus
15. Larry Doby

27. Their Niche Is Secure

1. Bob Feller, 1946
2. Duane Kuiper
3. Jim Lillie
4. Buzz Arlett
5. Russ Christopher
6. Stan Musial
7. Ted Lyons
8. Ike Butler
9. Eddie Plank, St. Louis Feds
10. Bill Klem
11. Pete Donohue
12. Jack Taylor
13. Steve Bedrosian
14. Vean Gregg
15. Pud Galvin

28. Minor League Maestros

1. Smead Jolley
2. Rabbitt Whitman
3. Steve Mesner
4. Fred Klobedanz
5. Howie "Howitzer" Moss
6. George Burns
7. Jimmy Walsh
8. Stony McGlynn
9. George Boehler
10. Lou "The Mad Russian" Novikoff
11. Spencer Harris
12. Pete Gray
13. Doc Crandall
14. Jack Bentley
15. Ox Eckhardt

AUGUST

The Magic Year
Stan Musial, 1948
29. Black Is Beautiful

1. Suitcase Simpson
2. Vida Blue
3. Cubs, 1953, Ernie Banks and Gene Baker
4. Josh Gibson
5. Tommy Davis
6. Sandy Nava
7. Luke Easter
8. Ellie Howard, 1963
9. John Lloyd
10. 1962
11. George Stovey
12. Jose Mendez
13. Padres, Johnny Grubb
14. Jackie Robinson, Montreal, 1946
15. Sam Jethroe, for the Braves, of course, not the Red Sox

30. Fabled Freshmen

1. Tim Raines, 1981
2. Remy Kremer
3. Steve Gerkin
4. Joe Hoover
5. Harvey Kuenn, 1953
6. Thurman Munson, 1970 and 1976 (Bit tricky, but subsequently means later, and Fred Lynn didn't win one later; he won his MVP the *same* year he took rookie honors.)
7. Goldie Rapp
8. Mike Griffin
9. Bob Grim
10. Abner Dalrymple, 1878
11. Pete Browning
12. Frankie Frisch
13. Dodgers, 1979–81; Sutcliffe, Howe, and Valenzuela
14. Pirates
15. Billy Rhines
16. Kevin Seitzer

31. Moments to Remember

1. John Miller
2. Glenn Wright
3. Willie Wilson
4. Joe Boehling
5. Barney McCosky
6. Johnny Mize, 1953
7. Richie Ashburn
8. Stan Musial
9. Dale Murphy, 1982–83
10. Larry Jackson
11. Ken Boyer and Tim McCarver
12. Nap Lajoie
13. Mike Schmidt
14. Joe Kohlman
15. Tommy Bond

32. Team Teasers

1. 1953 Dodgers
2. 1975–76 Reds
3. 1973 Mets
4. 1977–78 Yankees, Lou Piniella
5. 1920 White Sox, Red Faber, Claude Williams, Eddie Cicotte, and Dickie Kerr
6. Red Sox
7. Gaylord Perry
8. 1910 White Sox
9. Indians
10. Carl Mays, 1918 Boston Red Sox
11. 1909, Pirates and Cubs
12. 1930 Phillies
13. Boston Beaneaters or Braves, 1897–98, 1905–06
14. Pirates, 1901–03
15. Red Sox, 1954–55

33. The Evolving Game

1. 1893; the surveyor misread the blueprint which read 60′ 0″ and had already built the mounds 60′ 6″ distant before the error was caught.
2. 1904
3. 1962
4. Games on Sunday, beer sold in its parks, 25¢ general admission ticket, half of the NL's 50¢ minimum
5. Chris Von der Ahe and Ted Sullivan
6. 1903, 1900 in NL
7. Pittsburgh, 1934
8. Diamond
9. Germany Schaefer
10. Will White
11. 1885
12. The right to substitute for any player at any time
13. All would have won bat crowns under today's rules.
14. Last time the Series was the best 5-of-9 instead of 4-of-7 games
15. 1969

34. Men of Mystery

1. Beau Bell
2. Bill Hoffer
3. Jay Kirke
4. Roy Cullenbine
5. Monte Kennedy
6. Bill Keister
7. Dan Meyer
8. Bob Dillinger
9. Bunk Congalton
10. Deron Johnson
11. Bruno Haas
12. Nixey Callahan
13. Mike Donlin

35. Their Niche Is Secure

1. George Brett, 1979
2. Phil Niekro
3. John Vukovich
4. Johnny Burnett
5. Denny McLain
6. Al Crowder
7. Dupee Shaw
8. Ron Guidry, 1978
9. George McBride
10. Gorman Thomas
11. Rube Waddell
12. Honus Wagner, Harry Steinfeldt
13. Enzo Hernandez
14. Bob Gibson
15. Harry Heilmann

SEPTEMBER

Only Yesterday
San Francisco, Seals Stadium, Joe Gordon,
Albie Pearson
36. Like Father Like Son

1. Eddie Collins
2. Dale Berra
3. Herman and Duane Pillette
4. Roy Smalley, Sr., and Jr.
5. Ducky and Dick Schofield
6. Earl Caldwell
7. Dolf and Doug Camilli
8. Earl and Bud Sheely
9. Joe Schultz, Sr., and Jr.
10. Len Gabrielson and son Len
11. Ewart "Dixie" Walker, sons Dixie and Harry
12. Howard and Dick Wakefield
13. Ray Grimes, son Oscar, and brother Roy
14. Gil and Ricardo Torrez
15. Ray and Bob Boone

37. South of the Border

1. Al Lopez
2. Zoilo Versalles, 1965
3. Hi Bithorn
4. Connie Marrero, Julio Moreno, Sandy Consuegra, and Camilio Pascual
5. Luis Aparicio
6. 1972, Dave Concepcion and Bert Campaneris, Reds and A's
7. Chico Ruiz
8. Rod Carew, 1969
9. Armando Marsans
10. Orlando Cepeda, 1958
11. Tony Perez
12. Bobby Estalella
13. Felix Millan
14. Mel Almada
15. Bobby Avila

38. World War II Wrinkles

1. Lou Boudreau
2. Van Lingle Mungo
3. Chuck Workman
4. Joe Kuhel, Stan Spence
5. Larry French
6. Johnny Dickshot and Tony Cuccinello
7. Bill Voiselle
8. Joe Heving
9. Mickey Livingston
10. Stan Musial and Walker Cooper
11. Bob and Roy Johnson
12. Bob Elliott

39. Now Batting for ...

1. Dave Philley
2. Sheriff Harris
3. Schoolboy Rowe
4. Red Lucas
5. Russ Snyder
6. Bud Stewart
7. Merv Rettenmund
8. Johnny Frederick
9. Jack Doyle
10. Dusty Rhodes
11. Gordy Goldsberry
12. Red Schoendienst
13. Jackie Mayo
14. Jerry Lynch

40. Their Niche Is Secure

1. Ted Simmons
2. Johnny Kling
3. Lyman Lamb
4. Matt Alexander
5. Milt Pappas
6. Don Sutton
7. Babe Ruth and Cy Seymour
8. Sparky Anderson
9. Spike Shannon
10. Ted Wilks
11. Max Carey
12. Tim Raines
13. Jimmy Sexton
14. Harmon Killebrew
15. Bobby Bonds
16. Nolan Ryan, 1987

41. Glorious Glovemen

1. Bill Mazeroski
2. Bill Rariden
3. Pat Moran
4. Don Money
5. Baby Doll Jacobson
6. Jimmy Austin
7. Harlond Clift
8. Bill Shindle, Ron Santo
9. Ray Jablonski
10. Graig Nettles
11. Richie Ashburn
12. Everett Scott, Lou Boudreau, and Luis Aparicio all are tied; credit for any one of the three; super if you got 'em all.
13. Eddie Collins
14. Ray Schalk
15. Amos Strunk

42. Minor League Maestros

1. Bunny Brief
2. Les Fleming
3. San Dungan
4. Murray Franklin
5. Bob Lennon
6. Jigger Statz
7. Herb Conyers
8. Ferris Fain
9. John Gochnauer
10. Paul Wachtel, Joe Pate, and Gus Johns
11. Ollie Carnegie
12. Reb Russell
13. John Monroe
14. Steve Bilko
15. Rocky Nelson

OCTOBER

Forgotten Series Hero
Casey Stengel, New York Giants and New York
Yankees, 1923 (When both still played in the
Polo Grounds)
43. October Heroes

1. Freddy Parent
2. Johnny Podres; won the game that gave the Dodgers their lone World Championship in Brooklyn.
3. Kent Tekulve, 1979 Pirates
4. The Fordham Flash— Frankie Frisch
5. Gene Bearden, Cleveland
6. Al Kaline
7. Joe McGinnity, 1904 Giants
8. Hoss Radbourne, 1884 Providence
9. Mule Haas; 1929 A's
10. Babe Adams, 1909 Pirates
11. Reggie Jackson, 1977 Yankees
12. Gary Templeton and Alan Wiggins, 1984 Padres
13. Willie Aikens
14. Monte Pearson
15. Connie Mack and Gabby Street, 1930–31

44. Their Niche Is Secure

1. Rogers Hornsby, Cubs, Braves, Cards, and formerly the Giants
2. Lefty Grove
3. Lu Blue
4. Lefty O'Doul
5. Eddie Stanky
6. Bucky Walters
7. Steve Stone, 1980; Urban Shocker, 27
8. Jim Bunning
9. Ed Walsh, 1908 White Sox, 40 but some say only 39
10. Rabbitt Maranville
11. Bobby Lowe and Monte Cross; Lowe was first to hit four homers in a game.
12. Addie Joss
13. Whitey Ford
14. Darrell Evans
15. Al Rosen and Eddie Mathews, 1953

45. October Heroes

1. Elmer Miller (not Whitey Witt)
2. Sherman Lollar
3. Clay Carroll, 1970
4. Whitey Ford, San Francisco (formerly New York) Giants
5. Hank Borowy
6. Johnny Kucks
7. Hank Gowdy
8. Bobby Grich and Brian Downing
9. Fernando Valenzuela, 1981
10. Howard Ehmke
11. Jimmy Sebring
12. Blue Moon Odom
13. Vic Wertz, Willie Mays
14. Jim Konstanty, 1950
15. Chris Chambliss, 1976, Mark Littell

46. North of the Border

1. Tip O'Neill
2. Frank "Blackie" O'Rourke
3. Quiet Joe Knight
4. Ken Mackenzie and Ray Daviault
5. Roland Gladu
6. Paul Hodgson
7. Jeff Heath
8. Fred Lake
9. Claude Raymond
10. 1983
11. Oscar Judd
12. Frenchy Bordagaray
13. Tecumseh Stars

47. Great Goats and Victims

1. Clarence and Dale Mitchell
2. Eric Show
3. Charlie Sweeney
4. Sherry Smith
5. Bill Hutchinson
6. Jose DeLeon
7. Bill Bevens
8. Orlie Weaver
9. Herb Score, Gil McDougald
10. Terry Felton
11. Pep Young
12. Mickey Cochrane
13. Les Sweetland
14. Elmer Myers and Joe Bush
15. Heinie Wagner

48. Death in the Afternoon

1. Ross Youngs
2. Ed Morris
3. Bugs Raymond
4. Harry Agganis
5. Marv Goodwin
6. Chick Stahl
7. Urban Shocker
8. Jim Doyle
9. Austin McHenry
10. Roberto Clemente

49. October Heroes

1. Lou Brock and Bob Gibson
2. Mark Koenig
3. Lew Burdette
4. Mickey Lolich
5. Dave Henderson
6. Chicken Wolfe
7. Jimmy Wilson
8. Larry Sherry, 1959
9. Jim Burton
10. Tony Lazzeri, Carl Hubbell
11. Red Faber, 1917
12. Curly Ogden, George Mogridge, Bucky Harris and John McGraw
13. Jim Lefebvre, 1966, Dodgers
14. Jim Bagby, Elmer Smith, Bill Wambsganss
15. Thurman Munson and Joe Morgan both fit the description on all counts, and since you were forewarned that something strange was afoot, you need both to score. The year: 1976, of course.

⌀ **SIGNET** (0451)

FOR THE SPORTS FAN . . .

☐ **THE MEN OF AUTUMN** *An Oral History of the 1949–1953 World Champion New York Yankees* **by Dom Forker.** With uncanny skill and accuracy Dom Forker recreates the days when Dimag was in center, Raschi was on the mound, the Yanks were winning another series, and all was right with the world. With a golden Yankee photo gallery.

(166590—$4.95)

☐ **THE COMPLETE HANDBOOK OF PRO BASKETBALL: 1990 EDITION edited by Zander Hollander.** The most comprehensive handbook available from opening tap to championship buzzer, it's like having 27 team yearbooks in one, plus a complete TV viewer's guide. Bird, Jordan, Magic, Wilkins, Stockton, Dumars, they're all here—with 300 profiles, 300 photos, schedules, rosters, scouting reports and career records. (162838—$5.95)

☐ **EVERYTHING YOU ALWAYS WANTED TO KNOW ABOUT SPORTS and Didn't Know Where to Ask by Mickey Herskowitz and Steve Perkins.** Here is the book that answers every question a sports fan ever had in the back of his mind and tells the truth about all the whispered rumors of the sports world. (124715—$2.75)

☐ **GREAT BASEBALL FEATS, FACTS & FIRSTS by David Nemec.** Thousands of scores, stats and stories in one amazingly complete volume! Discover the unconventional records, the offbeat feats, the historic scores and the one-of-a-kind characters that keep baseball flying—in this comprehensive up-to-the-minute encyclopedia. (161246—$4.95)

☐ **THE ULTIMATE BASEBALL QUIZ BOOK by Dom Forker.** A mound of tantalizing trivia for the baseball buff. You're up against a full count of questions about the American national pastime. See if you can touch all the bases, but look out! This newly revised edition just might throw you a curve! (152360—$4.95)

☐ **EAT TO WIN: The Sports Nutrition Bible by Dr. Robert Haas, with Foreword by Martina Navratilova.** In this #1 Nationwide bestseller, a world-class nutritionist reveals the secrets of the breakthrough diet that gives top athletes that unbeatable edge. "A winning recipe for energy, strength, speed and endurance!"—*The New York Times* (155092—$4.95)

*Prices slightly higher in Canada

Buy them at your local

bookstore or use coupon

on next page for ordering.

⊘ SIGNET (0451)

RIB TICKLERS!

☐ **HOW TO LIVE TO BE 100 OR MORE: The Ultimate Diet, Sex and Exercise Book by George Burns.** Let George Burns—the man who has a young mind and is taking a healthy body out to a disco tonight—be your guru, your guide and your uproarious entertainer in the book that tells you that you may get older, but you never have to get old!   (821785—$4.95)

☐ **MAD VERTISING, or Up Madison Avenue, An Accumulation of Asinine and Atrocious Advertising Approaches by Dick DeBartolo and Bob Clarke.** You've been duped, taken, swindled, cheated, lied to, conned, and abused by advertising for years! But now, for the *first time*, you are being offered a *real chance* to save money by buying this book (which just might save your life)!   (067398—$1.25)

☐ **1,001 GREAT ONE-LINERS by Jeff Rovin.** The greatest one-line jokes, observations, and commentaries, for the first time, put together as a source of information and inspiration for anyone who wants to brighten up a conversation, a speech, or a piece of writing. Instantly prepare and swiftly serve up a feast of laughter.   (164229—$3.95)

☐ **1,001 GREAT JOKES by Jeff Rovin.** Over 1,000 jokes, one-liners, riddles, quips and puns—for every audience and every occasion. Among the topics skewered in this collection are: bathrooms, yuppies, hillbillies, sex, small towns, weddings, writers and much more!   (159012—$4.50)

☐ **1,001 MORE GREAT JOKES by Jeff Rovin.** Once again we've set a new standard in the wittiest, wackiest, most outrageous in adult humor. Here are jokes for every occasion—from raising chuckles from friends and family, to rousing roars of laughter from all kinds of audiences. Even better, the jokes are organized alphabetically by subject—so open up this book for a nonstop feast of fun from A to Z.   (159799—$3.95)

☐ **THE OFFICIAL HANDBOOK OF PRACTICAL JOKES by Peter van der Linden.** A treasury of 144 rib-tickling tricks and leg-pulling pranks. This book will make your eyes water with laughter and the weirdest, wildest, most outrageously inventive and ingenious practical jokes ever assembled. Just make sure that when you read it, no one sees you doing it. Let them all learn about it the right way. The funny way.   (158733—$2.95)

Prices slightly higher in Canada

Buy them at your local bookstore or use this convenient coupon for ordering.

NEW AMERICAN LIBRARY
P.O. Box 999, Bergenfield, New Jersey 07621

Please send me the books I have checked above. I am enclosing $_____
(please add $1.00 to this order to cover postage and handling). Send check or money order—no cash or C.O.D.'s. Prices and numbers are subject to change without notice.

Name_____

Address_____

City _____ State _____ Zip Code _____

Allow 4-6 weeks for delivery.
This offer is subject to withdrawal without notice.

Ⓢ SIGNET BOOKS
(0451)

PLAY TO WIN!

☐ **BEGIN CHESS by D.B. Pritchard with a Foreword by Samuel Reshevsky.** A complete guide introducing the novice to the board, pieces, moves and the basic tactics and strategy of the game. Includes illustrative diagrams. (165187—$3.95)

☐ **SCARNE ON CARDS by John Scarne.** Acclaimed as "The Card Player's Bible," this book gives the complete rules of card games ranging from poker and blackjack to hearts and cribbage. Also describes professional cardshark tricks and sets guiding principles and central strategies that can make you a winner at the game of your choice.
(167651—$5.95)

☐ **SCARNE ON CARD TRICKS by John Scarne.** This volume includes 150 sure-fire time-tested, performance-perfected master card tricks. The tricks require no sleight-of-hand and are all explained and demonstrated. (158644—$4.50)

☐ **WINNING AT CASINO GAMBLING by Terence Reese.** A fascinating guide to the dos and don'ts of casino gambling. You'll learn everything from the basic rules of each game to the smartest bets to place and which to avoid. (159373—$3.95)

☐ **HOYLE'S RULES OF GAMES by Albert H. Morehead and Geoffrey Mott-Smith.** Revised edition. Authoritative rules and instructions for playing hundreds of indoor games. New bridge bidding and scoring rules.
(163095—$4.95)

Prices slightly higher in Canada

Buy them at your local bookstore or use this convenient coupon for ordering.

NEW AMERICAN LIBRARY
P.O. Box 999, Bergenfield, New Jersey 07621

Please send me the books I have checked above. I am enclosing $_____
(please add $1.00 to this order to cover postage and handling). Send check or money order—no cash or C.O.D.'s. Prices and numbers are subject to change without notice.

Name_____

Address_____

City _____ State _____ Zip Code _____
Allow 4-6 weeks for delivery.
This offer is subject to withdrawal without notice.